TEACHING STUDENTS TO BECOME HUMANITIES SCIENTISTS

BREAKING TRADITION OF LEARNING DIVIDES THROUGH DIGITAL HUMANITIES

VALIUR RAHAMAN

Made with ♥ on the Notion Press Platform
www.notionpress.com

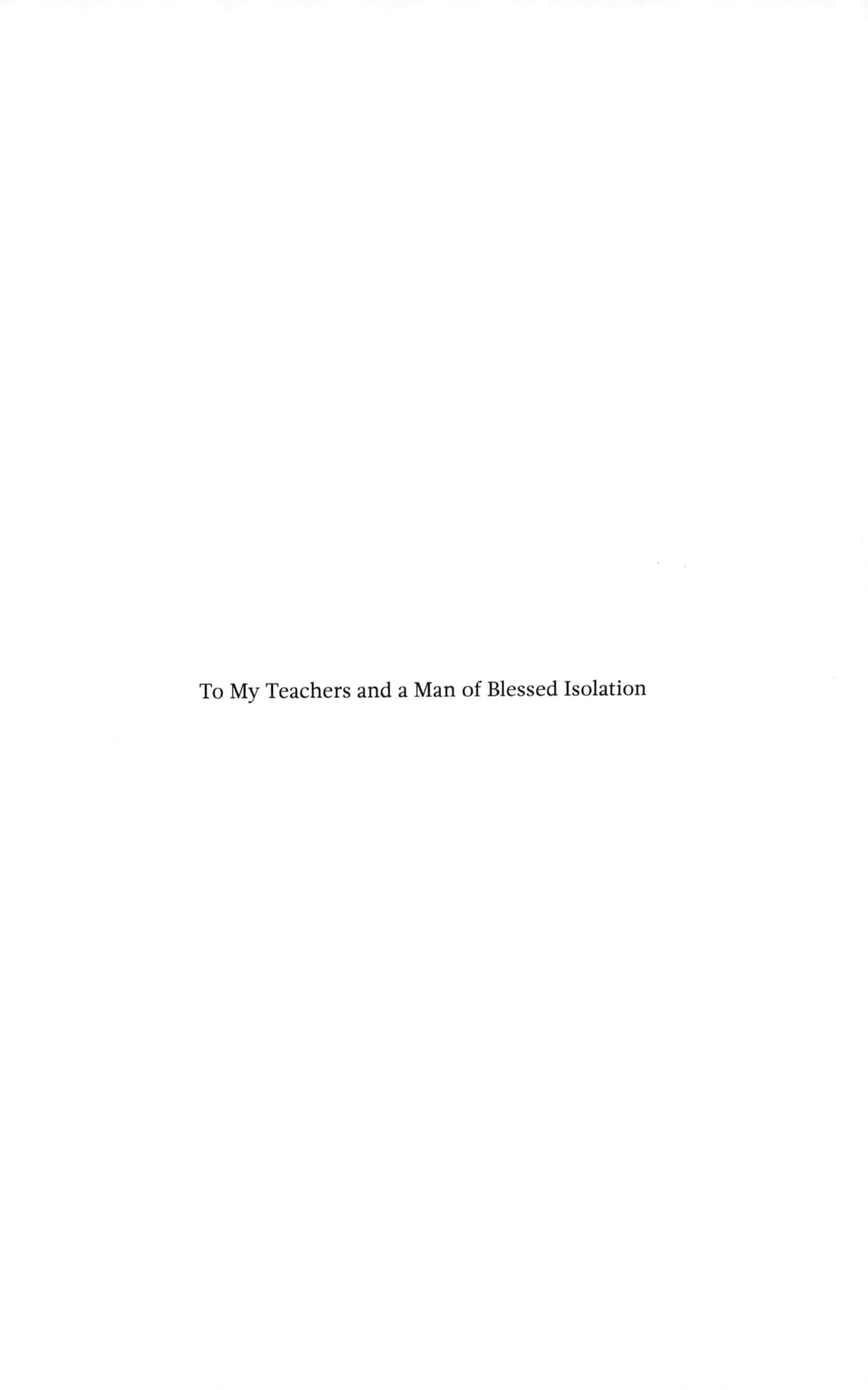

To My Teachers and a Man of Blessed Isolation

Contents

Foreword

Teaching Students to Become Humanities Scientists:Breaking Tradition of Learning Divides through Digital Humanities unlocks the power of Humanities through scientific inquiry.

In today's rapidly evolving academic landscape, the intersection of the humanities and scientific methodology offers a revolutionary approach to education. The book is a groundbreaking guide that empowers educators to integrate scientific principles with humanities disciplines, fostering a new generation of critical thinkers and innovative researchers.

Inside this transformative book, readers find:

- Innovative Pedagogical Strategies: Learn practical techniques for applying scientific methods to humanities subjects, including data analysis, experimental design, and empirical research.
- Illustrations from Real-World: Explore case studies and success stories from diverse educational settings where the integration of scientific inquiry has enriched the study of literature, history, philosophy, and the arts.
- Hands-On Activities: Access a range of classroom activities and assignments designed to engage students in interdisciplinary research and collaborative projects.
- Digital Tools and Resources: Get introduced to cutting-edge digital tools and resources that enhance the study and teaching of the humanities, from data visualization to digital archives.
- Assessment and Evaluation: Discover strategies for assessing student learning and progress in this innovative approach, ensuring that students not only grasp theoretical concepts but also apply them effectively.

Whether you are a seasoned educator, an academic researcher, or an enthusiastic advocate for interdisciplinary teaching, this book provides you with the insights and tools needed to inspire and challenge students. By bridging the gap between the humanities and the sciences, this book offers a fresh perspective on education that prepares students for the complexities of the modern world.

Join the movement to redefine humanities education and empower your students with the skills they need to excel in a multifaceted global landscape. Dive into *Teaching Students to Become Humanities Scientists:Breaking Tradition of Learning Divides through Digital Humanities* and start transforming your classroom today!

Preface

In the rapidly evolving landscape of academia, the fusion of technology and the humanities has opened up new dimensions of inquiry and expression. *Teaching Students to Become Humanities Scientists: Breaking Tradition of Learning Divides through Digital Humanities* is crafted to guide educators and students through the dynamic intersection of digital methodologies and traditional humanistic study. This book is an exploration of how we can effectively teach and engage with the growing field of digital humanities, preparing students to thrive as scholars who harness both humanistic insights and technological tools.

Purpose and Vision

Teaching digital humanities means teaching both technology and humanities on a platform. The basic problem is to teach lessons which are supposed to be learnable through practice, action and participation. DH is a research-based discipline that includes all the domains of knowledge. It has many extensions, threads, and many convergences which pull and push your attention critically. It needs a framework. In India, where we have yet not understand the technology its uses in other domains is a challenging task. Teaching is not a process of practising what is being taught but a channel through which students visualize beyond the matters of teaching. Hence, I decided to provide a comprehensive framework for teaching digital humanities with a focus on outcome-based education to visualize both related to decided and attained outcomes and beyond them (I mean mix hobby with the learning outcomes). Our vision is to equip educators with the strategies, tools, and pedagogical approaches needed to foster a new generation of humanities scientists—scholars who are adept at integrating digital techniques into their research and teaching. As the digital age transforms how we approach knowledge and inquiry, this book aims to bridge the gap between traditional humanities disciplines and contemporary technological practices. There are twelve chapters on various DH teaching-learning issues, problems and solutions.

Chapter 1 "Towards Designing Outcome-Based Courses in Digital Humanities" explors the principles of outcome-based education and how they can be applied to digital humanities. This chapter provides a foundation for designing courses that align educational objectives with the needs and skills required in the digital age. Chapter 2 "Humanities Scientist as a Career Goal" delves into the evolving role of the humanities scientist and the career opportunities that arise from integrating digital methods into humanistic research. It aims to inspire students by outlining the diverse pathways available in this interdisciplinary field. Chapter 3 "Teaching History of Digital Humanities" offers a comprehensive overview of the field's evolution, highlighting key milestones and influential figures. Chapter 4 "Teaching Digital Humanities Projects, Platforms, and Tools" provides practical guidance on how to teach students to engage with various digital humanities projects and tools. This chapter covers essential platforms and methodologies, equipping students with hands-on experience. Chapter 5 "Teaching Markup and Hypertext Markup Language (HTML)" presents how Markup languages are fundamental to digital text analysis and presentation. This chapter focuses on teaching the basics of HTML and its applications within digital humanities projects. Chapter 6 "Teaching Classification and Systems Theories" elucidates that classification and systems theories are integral for organizing and analyzing digital humanities data. This chapter explores methods for teaching these concepts and their relevance to effective data management and interpretation. Chapter 7 "Teaching Data and Databases" justifies how Data management is a cornerstone of digital humanities research. This chapter covers techniques for teaching database design, implementation, and analysis, emphasizing their application in humanities research. Chapter 8 "Teaching Data Narrative and Storytelling Frameworks" offers strategies for teaching students how to use data storytelling frameworks to create engaging and informative digital content. Chapter 9 "Teaching Information Visualization (InfoViz)" provides insights into teaching the principles and practices of data visualization, including tools and techniques for creating impactful visual representations. Chapter 10 "Teaching Data Mining and Text Analysis" argues that Data mining and text analysis are crucial for extracting insights from large datasets. This chapter explores methods for teaching these techniques and their application in humanities research. Chapter 11 "Teaching Text Encoding Initiatives (TEI)" covers the basics of TEI and its importance for encoding and interpreting historical and literary texts. Chapter 12 "Teaching Interface as Cross-Cultural Metaphor" addresses the challenges and strategies for teaching interface design with a focus on cross-cultural considerations, ensuring that digital tools are accessible and meaningful to diverse user groups. This book is seqal to *A Textbook on Databases in Digital Humanities* published by Notion Press. Chennai. India 2024<https://notionpress.com/read/a-textbook-on-databases-in-digital-humanities-hardcover>. And, another *Introducing Digital Humanities (* (2015)*<https://www.amazon.in/Introducing-Digital-Humanities/dp/9385528327>, 2nd Edition, Notion Press. 2024* (Forthcoming).

Cite this book: Rahaman, Valiur. *Teaching Students to Become Humanities Scientists: Breaking Tradition of Learning Divides through Digital Humanities.* Notion Press. Chennai. 2024. (MLA)

Looking Ahead

As I explore these chapters, it becomes clear that teaching digital humanities requires a nuanced understanding of both humanistic scholarship and technological innovation. By integrating these elements, we prepare students to engage with the complexities of modern research and to contribute meaningfully to the field. This book is intended to be a valuable resource for educators and learners committed to advancing digital humanities education. I hope that it will inspire new approaches to teaching and learning, foster interdisciplinary collaboration, and ultimately support the development of scholars who are equipped to navigate and shape the future of the humanities.

Thank you for joining us on this journey through the digital transformation of the humanities. May this book serve as a guide and inspiration as we collectively embrace the opportunities and challenges of teaching and learning in this exciting and evolving field.

Contact the author for an intensive teacher training/FDP on the topics covered in this book at <valiur.bsb@gmail.com>.

Valiur Rahaman

05 September, 2024

Email: valiur.bsb@gmail.com

Acknowledgements

The completion of this book, *Teaching Students to Become Humanities Scientists: Breaking Tradition of Learning Divides through Digital Humanities*, is the result of the collective efforts and insights of numerous individuals and institutions. First of all I convey profound admiration to to my wife and children for their immense support, compassion and blessed tolerance. I extend my deepest gratitude to mentors whose guidance and encouragement have been invaluable throughout this journey. I am thankful to Professor M.M. Salunkhe, Former Vice-Chancellor of Central University of Rajasthan for his discussion on the possible intersectionality between technology and education/literature /OBE education (2013-14), and for his apt guidance to statistical study of slow learners in the university, Professor G.R. Sinha, Vice-Chancellor of GSFC University, Vadodara for accepting collaborative works in digital humanities (2020), Professor R.K. Pandit Vice Chancellor MITS (Deemed University) for encouraging value added course proposals on digital humanities, and Professor Sanjay Modi, Pro-Vice Chancellor of Lovely Professional University, Punjab for supporting the ideas on implementing DH as a course component.

Special thanks to the students and educators who shared their experiences and perspectives, enriching the discussions and examples within these pages. Their dedication to exploring and expanding the boundaries of the humanities has been a constant source of inspiration. I also thank colleagues and friends who deny the relevance of digital humanities to traditional courses.

V.R.

Prologue

Yuvanne is an undergraduate student. She chose the DH course as an elective basket. I observed her activities during lecture delivery and practical sessions. She is now in the fourth semester with dissatisfaction with the chosen program as it is different from what she has done in the last schoolings. "What's your hobby," I asked her. "Hairstyling," she said. I was surprised to hear the unexpected answer. "What are you doing in the class of databases, then?" I asked. "Because it is prescribed and assigned, sir." She replied. I proposed to her an idea: "Can you develop the Girl's Hairstyling Online Platform and Management System?" I enquired. She was happy with the idea and now started taking an interest in database activities and has started enlisting types of locks and stylings One of the central themes of this book is the integration of disciplinary boundaries. It was a magical change. It was a spell of intersectionality between fashion communication and technology in the Digital Humanities classroom. I refer myself to re-read "Critical Pedagogy in Digital Era: Understanding the Importance of Arts & Humanities for Sustainable IT Development." See this paper at <https://papers.ssrn.com/sol3/papers.cfm?abstract_id=3387020> co-authored with Professor R.K. Pandit, and presented at AICTE Headquarters Delhi hosted ICDP conference in 2019. We presented an argument on mingling learners' hobbies with learning/course/programme outcomes and Polymodel Lab (Pundit & Rahaman 2019). The paper argues for critical pedagogy as a cross-disciplinary approach to teaching and research in Higher Education, focusing on the intersection of Arts and Humanities and Information Technology. It argues that IT should not replace Arts and Humanities, but rather help create a better society where machines and humans co-exist. The development of IT under the shadow of Arts and Humanities enriches both IT and human society. We shall see how reciprocal combining methods from the sciences with humanistic inquiry can lead to innovative research outcomes and provide richer insights into human phenomena. The interdisciplinary approach fosters a more holistic understanding of our world and opens up new avenues for exploration and discovery. The rise of digital humanities has revolutionized the way we approach research and teaching. Digital tools, including text analysis software, digital archives, and interactive visualizations, have expanded the possibilities for analyzing and presenting humanities data. Embracing these tools allows for greater accessibility and engagement, offering new ways to explore and interpret traditional texts and artefacts. To bring the change we have to break the the tradition of becoming monotonous in pedagogical approaches.

It does not mean that I do not favour the traditional way of teaching, but I favour upgrading the contents of the courses and introducing new pedagogies. Teaching students to become humanities scientists requires a shift in pedagogical practices. We have discussed strategies for incorporating scientific methods into humanities curricula, including project-based learning, data-driven research, and collaborative interdisciplinary projects. These strategies are designed to enhance critical thinking, foster creativity, and prepare students for the evolving demands of academia and beyond. At the heart of the humanities lies a commitment to critical thinking and ethical inquiry. As we adopt scientific methods and digital tools, it is crucial to maintain these core values.

This book has emphasized the importance of balancing technological advancements with ethical considerations and critical analysis to ensure that research and teaching practices remain grounded in humanistic principles.

This book is an outline only. A humble attempt to say, "We can experiment with new content to give new career pathways to students. Description is yet to come in the next book *DH Tools to Become Humanities Scientists.*

Valiur Rahaman
05 September, 2024
Email: valiur.bsb@gmail.com

CHAPTER ONE

Towards Designing Outcome-Based Course in Digital Humanities

Technology is an honest being without feelings unless you become dishonest with it.

-Dr Rahamat Ali MRCP

"If you devise a course in digital humanities, you will be out from the department of English." A head of nobody in a department threatened me. I was afraid. In fearful symetry of myself, I devised a course, and wrote the third book on the application of DH to practice NEP at large. He is unknown to the fact that now English has become technologized fully. All languages and all analyses are being assisted with AI based modelings. It does not mean that languages are dead now. But, it offers a unique opportunity to work in domains of aesthetics and technology. Who will work in this field like LLMs? Of course the people of Humanities and Social Sciences. We have to visualize that future humanities scientists. Outcome-based education (OBE) follows a simple rule: first, set the goal/career pathways, then create the course content with learning outcomes. OBE ensures students are well-prepared for future roles and responsibilities (Spady). Digital Humanities prioritises it.

Introduction

Let us understand the vision and mission of Digital Humanities. *The Digital Humanities Manifesto 2.0*, a collection of nine seminars co-taught by Jeffrey Schnapp and Todd Presner, was released by the UCLA Mellon Seminar in Digital Humanities. It declares:

Digital Humanities is not a unified field but an array of convergent practices that explore a universe in which: (a) print is no longer the exclusive or the normative medium in which knowledge is produced and/or disseminated; instead, print finds itself absorbed into new, multimedia configurations; and (b) digital tools, techniques, and media have altered the production and dissemination of knowledge in the arts, human and social sciences. The Digital Humanities seeks to play an inaugural role with respect to a world in which universities—no longer the sole producers, stewards, and disseminators of knowledge or culture—are called upon to shape natively digital models of scholarly discourse for the newly emergent public spheres of the present era (the www, the blogosphere, digital libraries, etc.), to model excellence and innovation in these domains, and to facilitate the formation of networks of knowledge production, exchange, and dissemination that are, at once, global and local. ("The Digital Humanities Manifesto 2.0," 2009).

Digital humanities (DH) uses various technologies and fields like literature, philosophy, and psychology to create human-readable, aesthetically dazzling works. Data in DH is subjective and interpretive, backed by quantitative and computational methods. The challenge is to transform a "thing" into something with informational and social value. Digital Humanities (DH) is a countercultural approach that challenges power structures and norms, promoting social justice and questioning the world. It requires expertise in content fields and technological methods and is inclusive of nonexperts and online crowds. DH involves experimentation, theorizing, research, data collection, content curation, data processing, and open publishing. Practitioners focus on diversity and exploration, with DH still emerging as an exploratory and provisional approach.

Creating and Criticizing Literary Corpora

Teaching DH provides a detailed description of the methodology used in a research project titled "Representations of oral varieties of language in the literature of the English-speaking world." The project aims to compile and analyze a corpus of literary prose texts, focusing on non-standardized linguistic features. The chapter addresses three topics of interest to the field of Digital Humanities: creating a digital corpus from printed source texts, corpus annotation, and qualitative and quantitative data analysis (Garside). The project uses a corpus of literary texts as a working example, focusing on the creation of a digital corpus, scanning practices, converting images into digital text, and proofreading the digital text. The chapter also discusses the use of Optical Character Recognition (OCR) to render the scanned text machine-readable.

Content and Sentiment Analysis

Content analysis is a method for making inferences from observed communications to their context. It involves replicable and valid methods, including conventional, directed, and summative approaches. Content analysis requires internal and external validity, which can be product or process-oriented. It is a versatile technique that can be adapted in various areas. The growing number of blogs and social networks has generated new opportunities and challenges for using information technologies to seek out and understand people's opinions and sentiments. Opinion mining is a discipline at the crossroads of information retrieval and computational linguistics, used in various applications. Sentiment analysis evaluates the polarity of specific information in a document through scoring or tagging. Opinion mining and sentiment analysis can work together in dealing with the computational treatment of opinion and subjectivity in text. Integrated sentiment analysis (iSA) combines sentiment analysis and opinion mining to create a new method, providing approximately unbiased estimates of category proportions even when the optimal classifier performs poorly. Sentiment analysis is increasingly relevant in the context of social media and social networks, particularly online social networks (OSNs). These platforms have transformed communication and have attracted academic researchers due to their affordability and reach. Common characteristics of OSNs include constructing public or semi-public profiles, articulating a list of users with whom they share connections, and viewing and traversing connections. The unique aspect of OSNs is not meeting strangers but enabling users to articulate and make visible their social networks. Network analysis is a methodology for analyzing social and interpersonal relations, and understanding degrees of separation is crucial for this manuscript. Orange and Voyant are two suitable for DH beginners (Baayen).

Teach Graph theory for this purpose. It is a useful tool for studying network connections, as it studies the connections between points in a network. Facebook and Twitter are examples of online social networks (OSNs) that are relevant for firms due to their virtual nature, high data availability, and the ability to provide emotional reactions. Sentiment analysis on OSNs can be a powerful tool, as they provide measurable emotional reactions generated by market players and users. However, the study focuses on the ability to analyze media messages using quantitative content analysis, which identifies the systematic assignment of communication content to categories and the analysis of relationships involving those categories using certain statistical methods. Instinctive sentiments, which identify emotional reactions without specific reasons, are considered, while rational sentiments identify reasoned responses. A model was developed to identify six areas: positive sentiment (positive sentiment), adhesion (positive sentiment), disapproval (negative sentiment), and aversion (negative sentiment). Instinctive sentiments measure attachment to the brand, while rational sentiments identify reasoned responses. Users who express positive sentiment can be classified into identification and adhesion areas, while users who express negative sentiment can be divided into disapproval and aversion areas. This model helps firms understand the emotional reactions generated by users and their interactions on social networks, allowing them to better understand and respond to their users‘ needs and preferences (Baayen).

OBE based DH Teaching

Outcome-Based Education (OBE)-based Digital Humanities (DH) teaching is an educational approach that focuses on defining and achieving specific learning outcomes in the field of Digital Humanities. It involves defining clear learning outcomes, aligning curriculum and assessment, and focusing on student-centred learning. The approach involves defining learning outcomes, designing curriculum, and using feedback and assessment results to continually improve teaching strategies and curriculum. Benefits of OBE-based DH teaching include clarity, focus, enhanced student learning, improved accountability, measurable results, and adaptability. Challenges include defining outcomes, balancing resources, and maintaining flexibility. By focusing on clear objectives, practical applications, and continuous improvement, OBE-based DH teaching creates a more effective and responsive educational experience.

OBE: From Sir S. Radhakrishnan to APJ Abdul Kalam to William Spady and Others

OBE (termed and practised differently) has stemmed from Aryabhatt's philosophy (Plofker, Kim 2009)and Chanakya's speeches if we trace it in global history. I quote lines from a speech of Sir Sarvepalli Radhakrishnan delivered on the occasion of the first convocation of the Banaras Hindu University (BHU) in 1926, "Education to be complete must be human, it must include not only training of intellect but refinement of the heart and discipline of the spirit. No education can be regarded as complete if it neglects heart and spirit". In this speech, Radhakrishnan emphasized the holistic nature of education, advocating for an approach that goes beyond mere intellectual training to also cultivate moral and spiritual growth. This address reflects his broader educational philosophy, which integrates intellectual, moral, and spiritual development as essential components of a well-rounded education. In his *The Reign of Religion in Contemporary Philosophy* explores the profound relationship between religion and philosophy in contemporary thought. He argues that religion and philosophy are deeply intertwined, with philosophy often reflecting religious values and concerns. Radhakrishnan examines how contemporary Western philosophers have been influenced by religious ideas, such as existentialist and phenomenological philosophies. He also critiques secularism, arguing that it fails to address the full spectrum of human experience. He advocates for dialogue between Eastern and Western philosophical traditions, recognizing that Eastern philosophies can enrich Western thought. Sir Radhakrishnan advocates for a unified approach to philosophy and religion, recognizing their complementary nature. In his *The Concept of Man: A Study in Comparative Philosophy* presents a comprehensive analysis of the concept of humanity across various philosophical and religious traditions. Radhakrishnan argues that each tradition provides unique insights into the nature of humanity, and a comparative approach allows for a deeper understanding. He emphasizes the importance of integrating Eastern and Western perspectives to gain a comprehensive view of humanity. Radhakrishnan also highlights the significance of spiritual and existential dimensions in understanding human nature. The book also explores human potential and self-realization, arguing that understanding these perspectives can help individuals realize their full potential. It also discusses the ethical and moral implications of different conceptions of humanity, arguing that philosophical and religious views influence ethical frameworks and moral values.

Sir Dr. A.P.J. Abdul Kalam, former President of India and aerospace scientist, wrote several influential books on various topics, including science, technology, spirituality, humanities, diplomacy, and leadership. His notable works include *Wings of Fire: An Autobiography*, *India 2020: A Vision for the New Millennium*, *Ignited Minds*, *The Life Tree*, *My Journey*, *Mission India*, *Turbulent Years*, *The Visionary*, *Strength of the Nation*, *You Are Born to Blossom*, *A Manifesto for Change*, and *Dreams 2 Destiny*. His books continue to inspire readers worldwide. I select *A Vision for the New Millennium* and *A Manifesto for Change* here to opine on his philosophy of teaching multidisciplinary subjects. He also has advocated for holistic education with new career pathways, and favoured intersectionality of interdisciplinary acadmism. A Vision for the New Millennium is a comprehensive and optimistic book that presents a forward-looking vision for India's future. It focuses on nation-building, economic growth, technological advancements, and sustainable development, emphasizing the need for strategic planning and execution. Kalam emphasizes the importance of investing in science and technology to drive economic growth and improve the quality of life for citizens. He advocates for educational reforms to enhance quality, accessibility, and relevance in the modern economy. The book also emphasizes the need to empower youth through education, skill development, and innovation opportunities. Sir Kalam emphasizes the importance of preserving and promoting India's rich cultural heritage, ensuring social justice and inclusivity, and promoting good governance. He advocates for visionary leadership and transparent, accountable, and efficient governance systems. Sir Kalam also emphasizes the importance of environmental stewardship, balancing development with ecological preservation, and promoting national unity and social harmony. He advocates for creating an environment that fosters scientific and technological innovation, investing in research and development to address global challenges. *A Vision for the New Millennium* presents a comprehensive and optimistic vision for India's future, focusing on leveraging education, technology, and leadership to drive national development while ensuring social justice and environmental sustainability.

His *A Manifesto for Change: A Sequel to India 2020* is a follow-up to his earlier work, *India 2020: A Vision for the New Millennium.* The book focuses on practical strategies and recommendations for achieving India's goals, including transformative leadership, quality education, economic development, social and rural development, sustainability, and environmental sustainability. Transformative leadership is essential for guiding India towards its goals, and effective leadership at various levels is crucial for driving change. The book emphasizes the importance of reforming the educational system to improve quality and relevance, promoting innovation, and promoting economic growth. Kalam advocates for educational policies that promote inclusive growth, ensuring that the benefits of economic development reach all sections of society, including marginalized communities.

These Indian works advocate for humanities-inspired academic developments I define it as holistic education. William Spady, a renowned educator, introduced the principles of Outcome-Based Education (OBE) in his influential book *Outcome-Based Education: Critical Issues and Answers* (1994) has also discussed holistic education prioritizing outcome-based career pathways. He developed Outcome-Based Education (OBE) as an educational framework in the 1980s and 1990s. He shifted the focus from traditional input measures to outcomes reflecting students' learning and abilities. His ideas emphasized achieving measurable goals aligned with real-world competencies and skills. Other educators and researchers, such as John Biggs and Grant Wiggins, have contributed to refining OBE principles. Biggs' Constructive Alignment concept emphasizes the alignment of learning outcomes, teaching activities, and assessments for effective learning. Wiggins and McTighe's work on backward design, outlined in their book Understanding by Design, has influenced the implementation of OBE by advocating for curriculum and assessments based on desired learning outcomes. While Spady is the key figure in OBE, other contributors have also played significant roles in shaping and applying the approach. As an educational approach, it defines measurable learning outcomes and designs the educational process to achieve them. It aligns teaching, assessment, and learning activities with specific goals or competencies. OBE promotes flexibility, and continuous improvement, and focuses on student learning, shifting from traditional input-based measures to actual achievement.

The Big Trio of OBE: William Spady, John Biggs and Grant Wiggins

Spady's work, particularly in the 1980s and 1990s, emphasized the importance of defining and measuring educational success based on specific, measurable learning outcomes rather than traditional evaluation methods. His work on OBE was widely discussed in articles and conference presentations, making it a crucial contribution to the field of education. Outcome-based education (OBE) is a system that focuses on what is essential for students to succeed in their learning experiences. This book explores the key issues related to understanding and implementing OBE, including its meaning, foundations, and relevance to global socioeconomic changes. It also discusses the meaning of outcomes and their derived meaning, four major trends in OBE, and the effects of different implementation approaches on students and schools. The book also clarifies common misconceptions about OBE and discusses future directions for OBE, highlighting its viability if democratic processes and strong professional norms prevail in society and education. The book concludes by discussing the future directions of OBE and its sustainability.

John Biggs, an Australian educational psychologist, is renowned for his work on "Constructive Alignment," which enhances curriculum design and teaching effectiveness in higher education. John Biggs' concept of Constructive Alignment is discussed in his influential works, such as *Teaching for Quality Learning at University* (co-authored with Catherine Tang) and "Aligning Teaching and Assessment to Curriculum Objectives," published in the *Assessment & Evaluation in Higher Education journal* in 2003. These works provide a comprehensive overview of how aligning learning outcomes, teaching activities, and assessment tasks can improve student learning and ensure all elements of coursework are together to achieve educational goals. Biggs' ideas on how to align teaching and assessment with learning outcomes and "Constructive Alignment in University Teaching" published in *HERDSA Review of Higher Education* in 2003 outline the principles of "Constructive Alignment" and its implications for teaching and learning. This approach helps create a coherent educational experience that enhances student learning and performance.

Grant Wiggins, co-author of *Understanding by Design*, has significantly influenced Outcome-Based Education (OBE) through his work on curriculum design and assessment. His contributions include the concept of "backward design," focusing on deep understanding, aligning assessments with learning outcomes, and providing a structured framework for curriculum development.

Hence, the Outcome-Based Education (OBE) concepts of William Spady, Grant Wiggins, and John Biggs focus on achieving effective learning outcomes. Spady's framework emphasizes defining clear, measurable outcomes, and promoting flexibility, accountability, and transparency. Wiggins' "backward design" approach focuses on fostering deep understanding and application of knowledge, while Biggs‘ Constructive Alignment aligns learning outcomes, teaching methods, and assessment methods to support effective learning. Spady promotes a broad approach, Wiggins provides a structured approach, and Biggs emphasizes student engagement. Each approach offers unique perspectives and methodologies, providing a comprehensive approach to effective outcome-based education.

The Other Two: Richard E. Mayer and Bloom's Taxonomy

Richard E. Mayer's multimedia learning principles, cognitive theories, and research-based instructional design contribute to the effectiveness of Open-Ended Education (OBE). These principles enhance instructional materials, facilitating better understanding and retention. Mayer's active learning approach and research-based instructional design ensure students are actively engaged in achieving learning outcomes. His work supports the goals of OBE by providing evidence-based strategies. Bloom's Taxonomy is an essential instrument in Outcome-Based Education (OBE) since it offers a systematic framework for identifying, organizing, and evaluating learning outcomes. The system arranges cognitive abilities in a structured order, guaranteeing well-defined goals and precise, quantifiable results. The taxonomy also facilitates the development of curriculum and instructional activities that are in line with the intended learning goals, fostering a wide range of learning experiences. Additionally, it guarantees consistency and precision in the instructional process, fostering a more profound comprehension and enhanced cognitive abilities.

Bloom's Taxonomy is named after Benjamin Bloom, an American educational psychologist who led a team of scholars in the mid-20th century to develop a framework for categorizing educational goals. Bloom's Taxonomy was first published in 1956 and has since become a foundational tool in education for defining and organizing learning objectives.

Benjamin Bloom (1913–1999)

Bloom was a prominent educational psychologist whose work focused on developing ways to classify and assess educational objectives. His leadership in creating the taxonomy has had a lasting impact on curriculum design, teaching, and assessment practices.

The Original Taxonomy (1956)

The original version, often referred to as Bloom's Taxonomy, categorized cognitive skills into six levels of increasing complexity: Knowledge, Comprehension, Application, Analysis, Synthesis, and Evaluation. This framework was designed to help educators create more effective and organized educational goals and assessments.

Revised Taxonomy (2001)

In 2001, a revision of Bloom's Taxonomy was published, led by Lorin Anderson and David Krathwohl, among others. This revised version updated the original categories to better reflect modern educational practices and understanding. The revised taxonomy consists of:

1. Remembering: Retrieving, recognizing, and recalling relevant knowledge.
2. Understanding: Constructing meaning from instructional materials.
3. Applying: Using knowledge in new situations.
4. Analyzing: Breaking information into parts and examining relationships.
5. Evaluating: Making judgments based on criteria and standards.
6. Creating: Putting elements together to form a new coherent whole.

Purpose and Impact

Educational Goals

Bloom's Taxonomy helps educators define clear and measurable learning objectives by categorizing different levels of cognitive skills, from basic recall of facts to higher-order thinking.

Curriculum Design

It provides a structured approach to designing curriculum and instructional activities that target various levels of cognitive complexity, ensuring a comprehensive educational experience.

Assessment Development

The taxonomy aids in developing assessments that align with educational goals, allowing educators to evaluate student learning across different levels of cognitive skills.

Key Aspects of Outcome-Based Education

OBE is an educational approach that focuses on defined learning outcomes, curriculum alignment, and assessment methods. See the figure 1.

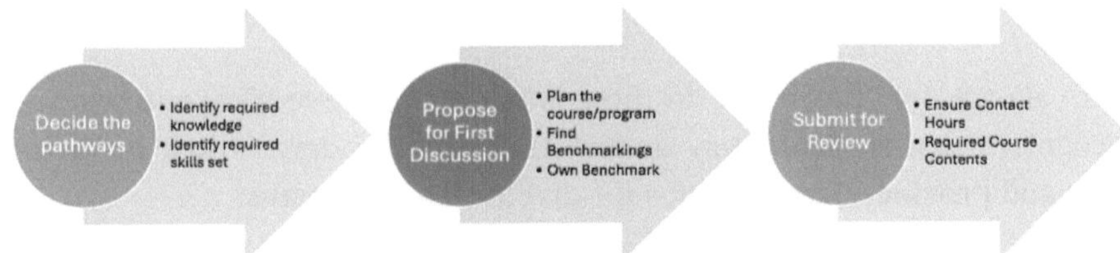

Figure 1: Initial Process of Desiging a OBE Course/Program

It allows flexibility in learning, emphasizes student-centred learning, encourages continuous improvement, and enhances accountability and transparency by ensuring that education is relevant and meaningful to students' needs and goals. Based on the initial process, educator can observe the key aspects of OBE based course/program:

a. Defined Outcomes

OBE starts with clearly defined learning outcomes or competencies that students are expected to achieve by the end of an educational program or course. These outcomes are specific, measurable, and aligned with the goals of the educational institution or program.

b. Curriculum Alignment

The curriculum, including content, teaching methods, and learning activities, is designed to help students achieve the specified outcomes. This alignment ensures that all aspects of the educational experience contribute to reaching the defined goals.

c. Assessment Methods

Assessments are designed to measure whether students have achieved the learning outcomes. These assessments can be formative (ongoing and used to provide feedback during the learning process) or summative (used to evaluate overall achievement at the end of a course or program).

d. Flexibility in Learning

OBE allows for flexibility in how students achieve the outcomes. It recognizes that students may demonstrate their understanding in various ways and provides opportunities for diverse learning paths.

e. Student-Centered Learning

The approach focuses on student learning and achievement rather than simply the delivery of content. It emphasizes what students can demonstrate and accomplish, ensuring that education is relevant and meaningful to their needs and goals.

f. Continuous Improvement

OBE encourages the use of data and feedback to continuously improve teaching practices and learning outcomes. Educators regularly review and adjust their methods based on assessment results and feedback from students.

g. Accountability and Transparency

By clearly defining outcomes and aligning assessments with these outcomes, OBE provides a transparent way to measure and demonstrate student progress and achievement. This enhances accountability for both educators and students.

The action verbs associated with each level of Bloom's Taxonomy help educators create clear and measurable learning objectives. These verbs specify the kinds of cognitive processes that students should demonstrate at each level of the taxonomy. A breakdown of action verbs for each level is given below:

1. Remembering (Recall and Recollection)

Action Verbs

1. Define
2. Describe
3. Identify
4. List
5. Name
6. Recognize
7. Recall
8. Retrieve
9. Repeat
10. State

2. Understanding (Comprehension)

Action Verbs

1. Classify
2. Compare
3. Contrast
4. Discuss
5. Explain
6. Express
7. Extend
8. Illustrate
9. Infer
10. Interpret
11. Paraphrase
12. Summarize

3. Applying (Use of Information)

Action Verbs

1. Apply
2. Demonstrate
3. Execute
4. Implement
5. Interpret
6. Operate
7. Perform
8. Solve
9. Use
10. Utilize

4. Analyzing (Break Down and Examine)

Action Verbs

1. Analyze
2. Break down
3. Compare
4. Contrast
5. Critique
6. Differentiate
7. Diagram
8. Distinguish
9. Examine
10. Investigate
11. Relate
12. Organize
13. Structure

5. Evaluating (Make Judgments)

Action Verbs

1. Appraise
2. Assess
3. Criticize
4. Defend
5. Evaluate
6. Judge
7. Justify
8. Rate
9. Recommend
10. Revise
11. Support

6. Creating (Synthesize and Generate)

Action Verbs

1. Adapt
2. Assemble
3. Construct
4. Create
5. Design
6. Develop
7. Formulate
8. Generate
9. Modify
10. Organize
11. Plan
12. Propose
13. Reconstruct
14. Synthesize

Using action verbs in education ensures clear, measurable learning goals, guiding students in achieving their objectives and facilitating the design of appropriate instructional activities and assessments. They help educators and learners understand the complexity of cognitive tasks and design appropriate learning experiences. Each level of the taxonomy builds on the previous one, requiring more complex thinking and deeper understanding. By using these action verbs, educators can clearly articulate learning objectives and assess student performance at various levels of cognitive processing. Following the above principles of OBE and designs an educator can develop DH courses. Understanding the value of multidisciplinary in humanities and social sciences domains, UGC may take the initiative to launch digital humanities as a programme at the UG and PG levels. NTA may offer NET-JRF in this course soon. It will boost the proposal of launching Digital Humanities as a programme which was forwarded in my book *Introducing Digital Humanities* and *A Textbook on Databases in Digital Humanities*. Digital is not free from control because humanities work from its side to remind the words of Sir S. Radhakrishnan "The importance of education is not only in knowledge and skill, but it is to help us to live with others." (Bhatia, S. & Sarin, A., 2004, p.239).

Works Cited and Recommended Readings

Bare Bones Software, TextWrangler. Available via http://www.barebones.com/products/ textwrangler.

David Michael Berry. Understanding Digital Humanities. Basingstoke, Palgrave Macmillan, 2012.

Jew, Shalin Hai- (eds.) Data Analytics in Digital Humanities. Springer International Publishing. 2017.

N. Levshina, How to do Linguistics with R. John Benjamins, Amsterdam, 2015.

Plofker, Kim. Mathematics in India. Princeton: Princeton University Press. 2009.

Percillier, Michael & Paulin, Catherine. A Corpus-based Investigation of World Englishes in Literature. World Englishes. 2016. Available at https://doi.org/10.1111/weng.12208.

R. Garside, The CLAWS word-tagging system, in The Computational Analysis of English: A Corpus-based Approach, ed. by R. Garside, G. Leech, G. Sampson (Longman, London, 1987), pp. 30–41

R.H. Baayen, Analyzing Linguistic Data. Cambridge University Press, Cambridge, 2008.

Radhakrishnan, S. The Reign of Religion in Contemporary Philosophy. Macmillan. London. 1920.

Radhakrishnan, S. *The Concept of Man: A Study in Comparative Philosophy*. Allen & Unwin. London. 1966.

Schillp, Paul Arthur. *The Philosophy of Sarvepalli Radhakrishnan*, Motilal Banarsidass, 1992. p. ix

Schreibman, Susan, et al. A New Companion to Digital Humanities. Wiley Blackwell. Copyright, 2016.

CHAPTER TWO

Humanities Scientist as a Career Goal

People say that AI has finished the sense of education and research. I deny this grapevine communication and rumour. I visualize a future when a Google-like company will seek the contribution of humanities scientists to upgrade and control the growing technology. A Humanities Scientist applies scientific methods to the study of human culture, history, languages, literature, arts and philosophy. They integrate methodologies from sciences or social sciences to investigate topics related to human culture, history, and languages. They work on interdisciplinary projects, digital humanities, empirical research, and scientific principles. They publish research and teach courses that integrate scientific approaches with humanities content, fostering innovative approaches to understanding human culture and history.

If you launch Digital Humanities as a Course?

'Digital Humanities'(Maniar; Chansanam et al.; Zilberg) is a rocket science for practitioners of humanities and social sciences. The phrase 'rocket science' is commonly used to refer to the fields of aerospace engineering and astrodynamics, which have germinated many new disciplines to utilize knowledge of science and technology to know the mysteries of the universe. Another reflection of the dictum "it's not rocket science" is that it is used to describe anything that is easily comprehensible. But, for teachers, trainers, students, and learners of Arts, Humanities, and Social sciences, digital humanities is a rocket science. I insist on saying this by observing low acceptance rates of 'humanities computing', 'computational humanities' or say 'digital humanities' (they have different relative meanings) or 'humanities-inspired technology' in the practices of its parent domain. It is quite natural because we had been in a war between two cultures: the culture of arts and science; and of humanities and technology, which has already been noted by C.P Snow, E.W. Wilson, and John Brockman. British scientist and novelist C. P. Snow delivered Rede Lecture on "The Two Cultures" in 1959, which was published in book form as *The Two Cultures and the Scientific Revolution*, John Brockman's *The Third Culture: Beyond the Scientific Revolution* (1995) explored Snow's ideas with a new concept of 'third culture'. The biologist Edward Osborne Wilson's *Consilience: The Unity of Knowledge* (1998) is an attempt to bridge the gap between "the two cultures".(Snow CP; Wilson; Rahaman) To challenge this bridgeless academism, new academic terminologies came into practices like interdisciplinary, crossdisciplinarity, multidisciplinary and trans-disciplinary yet low acceptance rates are noted due to what Snow termed "natural Luddites". It is, then, the responsibility of teachers to dissolve this luddite's bridgelessness by introducing the students to the latest research advancements and the power of academic synchronization to challenge the prevalence of technological/digital illiteracy that ultimately results in the global society of digital divide. Unless academic and research synchronization of various disciplines is practised, Digital humanities will remain a rocket science. So the word, 'rocket science' is used to refer to encompass distinctive, unrepresentable, inconclusive, ground-breaking, latest, unmodifiable, inadmissible, and similar words. It is rocket science for those who are not updated with recent advancements or do not embrace them because they are not ready to come outside the 'comfort zone' which is their choice of life or do not assess its requirements. For these reasons, students' progressive curiosity, choices and careers are damaged. Hence, a future generation is damaged and the vision of digital society, digital citizenship, digital marketing, and digital life are overlooked and damaged. And, if DH is comprehended once by humanities scholars, it will change the face of academics and research. A new era of transdisciplinary disciplines(Chowdhary and Rahaman; Pandit and Rahaman; Rahaman and Aftab) will be born to develop a new team for societal development. Outcome-based education has come to let realise the value of education, skills and feasibility of knowledge, and its monetization. Entrepreneur humanities is born out of OBE practices. (Rahaman et al.) Let me share some observations on the status of humanities in the world, and then will proceed with ideas on it.

Humanities was overlooked for half of the century in the name of irrelevant imaginative sentiments exposures, and platonic hates(Davidson and Goldberg; Berlowitz; Muller) ignoring the fact that it generates ideas of the years, controls the inhuman developments of technology, and asks to upgrade it for better human services by bringing forth the discourses oh human conditions. After the works of Roberto A Busa under the sponsorship of IBM in 1945-6, computing humanities came into being. With the publication of *Companion to Digital Humanities* and *Debates in Digital Humanities* in the USA, and *Introduction to Digital Humanities* in India, Digital Humanities became an incredible source of conserving, preserving, disseminating, accessing, and democratizing the human and posthuman knowledge system. In India, it was discussed at Central University of Rajasthan Ajmer during 2014-15 (Proposal to develop a new department of digital humanities), MITS Gwalior in 2019-20 (Value Added Course), and finally a course *Introduction to Digital Humanities* was launched at Lovely Professional University, for the very first time in 2023-24 in India. Digital humanities (DH) is an academic discipline that combines computing and digital technology with humanities subjects. It entails the methodical utilisation of digital resources and their examination, fostering collaborative, transdisciplinary, and computationally involved research, teaching, and publication. Digital humanities facilitates the adoption of innovative pedagogical approaches while evaluating their influence on cultural heritage and the digital realm. It fosters a reciprocal interaction between the humanities and digital technology.

Scholars and practitioners are continuously formulating the notion of the digital humanities. Given the dynamic and expanding nature of the industry, precise definitions might swiftly become obsolete or unduly restrict future possibilities. The acknowledgement of the challenge in delineating the scope of the field is seen in the second edition of Debates in the Digital Humanities (2016). "In addition to the previous focus on digital archives, quantitative analyses, and tool-building projects, the field of DH now includes a diverse range of methods and practises. These include creating visual representations of large image collections, using 3D modelling to study historical artefacts, producing dissertations in digital format, analysing hashtag activism and related activities, developing alternate reality games, setting up mobile maker spaces, and more." Defining the exact nature of digital humanities work can be challenging within the broad framework of what is known as a 'big tent' DH. (Zilberg)

The digital humanities originated from humanities computing and has since been linked to various disciplines, including humanistic computing, social computing, and media studies. The digital humanities encompasses a range of subjects, including the curation of online collections of primary sources, primarily consisting of text, as well as the analysis of massive cultural datasets through data mining techniques and topic modelling. Digital humanities encompasses the integration of both digitised and born-digital materials, merging the methodologies of traditional humanities disciplines (including rhetoric, history, philosophy, linguistics, literature, art, archaeology, music, and cultural studies) and social sciences with computational tools (such as hypertext, hypermedia, data visualisation, information retrieval, data mining, statistics, text mining, and digital mapping) and digital publishing. Additional subfields within the realm of digital humanities have surfaced, such as software studies, platform studies, and critical code studies. Related disciplines to the digital humanities include new media studies, information science, media theory of composition, game studies (especially about digital humanities project design and development), and cultural analytics. Every academic discipline and every nation possesses its distinct chronicle of digital humanities.(Tinits et al.; Varela et al.; Nagasaki)

The Digital Humanities Stack, as described by Berry and Fagerjord in their book *Digital Humanities: Knowledge and Critique in a Digital Age* refers to a collection of tools and technologies used in the field of Digital Humanities. Berry and Fagerjord propose the idea of reimagining digital humanities by employing a "digital humanities stack"(Berry and Fagerjord). They contend that "this particular diagram is prevalent in computation and computer science to illustrate the hierarchical arrangement of technologies, with each level of abstraction built upon the one below it."(Berry and Fagerjord) Here, the technique is employed more vividly and imaginatively to demonstrate the various activities, practises, abilities, technologies, and structures that constitute the digital humanities, to offer a comprehensive overview. The graphic represents the foundational components of the digital humanities stack, including computational thinking and knowledge representation at the lower levels, which serve as the basis for the subsequent aspects.(Berry and Fagerjord)

Practically speaking, a significant differentiation in the field of digital humanities lies in the emphasis placed on the data that is being analysed. When it comes to handling written information, digital humanities relies on a rich and extensive background in digital editing, computational linguistics, and natural language processing. It has also developed its own advanced technology stack, which is primarily based on the specifications of the Text Encoding Initiative. This specific section of the study is occasionally distinguished from Digital Humanities as 'digital philology' or 'computational philology'. Digital philologists utilise digital practises, methodologies, and technology, such as optical character recognition, to create and analyse digital versions of objects or artefacts. These tools allow them to adapt the field to the digital age(Berry and Fagerjord).

Why Technology for Humanities and Social Sciences?

Students in Humanities and Social Sciences are afraid of mathematics and computer science and therefore they of devoid of scientific and technological knowledge. They often lack mathematical skills, which tags them as incompetent to enter the field of technology and science.(Dubrovina et al.; Maniar; Schreibman et al.; Risam; Schiffrin and Michalska) It resulted in many places of technical illiteracy and partially literate educated people in technology. In that condition, it is essential to make them aware of technology education/training lack of which the country will lack a digital society and citizenship or digital crime will exceed more than expected and will leave helplessness with people.

Many students do not know about the domain and sub-domains. It is the responsibility of a teacher to let the students know about the parent domain, major domain, sub-domain, and career-oriented domains. For example, the students of political science do not know about parent schools and the major domains in them. They do not know about the terms 'humanities' and 'social sciences'; the difference between them, and intersections with other parent schools and domains. It is, therefore, important to sensitize students to know about the meaning, connections, and values of humanities. Digital humanities cannot be understood unless the term 'humanities' is comprehended.(Zilberg) Let us define humanities first. Humanities is the parent school of The field of digital humanities encompasses scholarly endeavors that include the convergence of digital technology and disciplines within the humanities. The designation "humanities" was initially employed during the Renaissance period by Italian scholars who were actively engaged in the examination and restoration of ancient works from classical antiquity. The above-mentioned word highlights the transition from a medieval Theo-centric perspective to a human-centred worldview when humanity is seen as the ultimate standard for all matters. The humanities encompass a range of academic disciplines that centre on the exploration and analysis of many forms of artistic expression, including but not limited to the arts, literature, music, dance, theatre, architecture, philosophy, and other manifestations of human civilization. However, the term “digital” pertains to what specific attribute or characteristic? Furthermore, what are the ramifications of the phrase for the tasks being executed inside this framework?

Career in the Humanities Science

A "Humanities Scientist" is not a standard term in academic disciplines, but I interpreted it on many occasions as someone who applies scientific methods, analytical techniques, or empirical research approaches to the study of the humanities. This role typically involves integrating methodologies from the sciences or social sciences to investigate topics related to human culture, history, languages, philosophy, and other areas traditionally considered part of the humanities. A Humanities Scientist is operative in:

1. Interdisciplinary Research

- Combining Methods: A Humanities Scientist might employ quantitative methods, data analysis, or experimental techniques to explore humanities questions. For example, they might use statistical analysis to study trends in historical data or apply computational methods to analyze large corpora of texts.
- Collaborative Projects: They often work on interdisciplinary projects that bridge the gap between humanities and sciences, such as digital humanities projects that involve data visualization, GIS (Geographic Information Systems), or machine learning.

2. Digital Humanities

- Technology Integration: In the field of digital humanities, Humanities Scientists use digital tools and technologies to analyze and interpret cultural and historical data. This can include text mining, digital archiving, and creating interactive visualizations.
- Innovation: They innovate new ways to study and present humanities research using digital methods, enhancing accessibility and engagement with historical and cultural content.

3. Empirical Research

- Data Collection: They might collect and analyze empirical data related to human behaviour, cultural patterns, or historical phenomena. For instance, using surveys or experiments to understand contemporary cultural trends or historical research methods to validate findings.
- Quantitative Analysis: Employing quantitative techniques to analyze patterns in literature, art, or historical records, such as statistical analysis of literary styles or trends over time.

4. Application of Scientific Principles

Scientific rigour involves applying rigorous methodologies from sciences to humanities research, ensuring robust, replicable, and evidence-based findings. Hypothesis testing involves formulating and testing hypotheses about cultural or historical phenomena using methods associated with the scientific method.

5. Academic Contributions

Publications: Publishing research that bridges humanities and scientific approaches, contributing to both fields and fostering new methodologies.

Teaching: Teaching courses that integrate scientific approaches with humanities content, helping students develop skills in both areas.

Career Choices and Works

- Historical Data Analysis: Using statistical methods to analyze large datasets of historical documents.
- Textual Analysis: Applying natural language processing to study literary trends and patterns.
- Cultural Analytics: Employing data visualization to map and analyze cultural phenomena across different regions or periods.
- Web development

Example of a Career in Data mining and developers

A career in data mining and development offers diverse opportunities and involves leveraging data to extract valuable insights and build solutions that can drive decision-making and innovation. Here's an overview of what such careers entail, the skills required, and potential career paths:

1. Data Mining

What It Involves

- Data Exploration: Identifying patterns and correlations in large datasets using statistical and computational techniques.
- Algorithm Development: Creating and applying algorithms to discover hidden patterns or insights in data.
- Predictive Modeling: Building models that can predict future trends based on historical data.
- Data Cleaning: Preparing and cleaning data to ensure accuracy and usability.

Set of Skills

- Statistical Analysis: Understanding and applying statistical methods to interpret data.
- Programming: Proficiency in programming languages such as Python, R, or SQL.
- Machine Learning: Knowledge of machine learning algorithms and frameworks.
- Data Visualization: Ability to present data findings effectively using tools like Tableau or Power BI.
- Data Handling: Experience with databases, data warehousing, and data management.

Career Paths

- Data Scientist: Focuses on analyzing complex data to generate actionable insights and build predictive models.
- Data Analyst: Works on interpreting data, creating reports, and visualizing data to support business decisions.
- Data Engineer: Designs and builds infrastructure for data generation, collection, and storage.
- Business Intelligence (BI) Developer: Develops and manages BI solutions and data visualization tools.

2. Developers

Software development involves designing, coding, and testing software applications for various platforms and devices. Web development involves creating and maintaining websites, while application development focuses on building and managing applications for specific business or user needs.

Skills Set

Proficiency in programming languages like Java, C++, Python, JavaScript, or Ruby, knowledge of software engineering methodologies like Agile and Scrum, database management skills like MySQL and MongoDB, experience with version control systems like Git, and strong analytical and problem-solving abilities.

Career Paths

- Software Developer: Creates software applications, writes code, and performs testing and debugging.
- Web Developer: Specializes in developing and maintaining websites and web applications.
- Mobile App Developer: Focuses on building applications for mobile platforms (iOS, Android).
- Full Stack Developer: Works on both front-end and back-end development, handling all aspects of software development.
- Systems Analyst: Analyzes and designs solutions to improve or upgrade existing systems.
-

Combining Data Mining and Development: Roles that Integrate Both Fields

Data Engineer: Combines skills in data mining and software development to build and maintain data infrastructure and pipelines.

Machine Learning Engineer: Develops and deploys machine learning models, requiring both data mining expertise and strong development skills.

Data Scientist: Often needs to write code and develop tools for data analysis, blending data mining with software development.

Educational Background and Qualifications

Ministry of Education, UGC and the government organization play crucial roles in deciding the required qualifications for recruitment in higher education, and affiliated or sister organizations. Typically, the required diploma/degree is a bachelor's or master's degree in fields such as Computer Science, Data Science, Statistics, or a related discipline. It also includes people from humanities and social science background who has the related skill sets. This will increase the intake of students for the same reasons.

Certifications

Relevant certifications can enhance credentials, therefore, Certified Data Professional (CDP), AWS Certified Data Analytics, or certifications from data science boot camps with BA, MA and MPhil/PhD in Humanities and Social Sciences are justifiable qualifications.

Experience

For such challenges, practical experience through internships, projects, or work experience in data analysis or software development is highly valuable, so it can be planned during the program design. Humanities Scientists may be given opportunities for industry applications:

1. Finance: Fraud detection, risk management, and investment analysis.
2. Healthcare: Patient data analysis, predictive modelling for treatment outcomes, medical narrative research.
3. Retail: Customer behavior analysis, inventory management.
4. Technology: Software development, user experience design, and data-driven product development.

A career in data mining and development offers the opportunity to work on impactful projects across various industries, leveraging data and technology to drive innovation and solve complex problems.

Learning Divides

I used learning divides in academics to refer to the gaps or disparities in educational outcomes, opportunities, and resources among different groups of learners. These divides can manifest in various forms and are influenced by a range of factors, including socioeconomic status, geographic location, access to technology, and educational policies. Understanding and addressing learning divides is crucial for promoting equity and ensuring that all students have the opportunity to succeed academically.

Types of Learning Divides

Academic Divide: Arts, Science, and Technology

The academic divide between arts, sciences, and technology refers to the differences in disciplines, methodologies, and educational approaches across these areas. Arts, including literature, visual arts, performing arts, history, and philosophy, emphasize creative expression, cultural understanding, and critical analysis. These fields typically employ qualitative methods, such as critical interpretation, historical analysis, and aesthetic evaluation. Science, including biology, chemistry, physics, and environmental science, focuses on understanding natural phenomena, conducting experiments, and applying scientific principles. These fields often employ empirical methods, such as experimentation, observation, and data analysis. Education in science typically includes laboratory work, quantitative analysis, and theoretical knowledge. Technology, including computer science, engineering, information technology, and applied sciences, focuses on designing, developing, and applying technological solutions to solve problems and improve systems. It employs quantitative methods and engineering principles, emphasizing practical application and innovation. Bridging the divide through interdisciplinary collaboration and integrated educational strategies can lead to innovative solutions and a more comprehensive understanding of complex problems. By recognizing and addressing the unique strengths and challenges of each discipline, educators and professionals can foster a more integrated and dynamic academic environment.

The academic divide between arts, sciences, and technology is a significant issue in education and research. It arises from several factors, including different focus and objectives, methodological differences, educational approaches and curriculum, resource allocation and funding, career paths and outcomes, cultural and institutional norms, and the need for interdisciplinary collaboration.

Arts focus on creativity, expression, and cultural interpretation, while sciences aim to understand natural phenomena through empirical research and the scientific method. Technology focuses on developing tools, systems, and processes to solve specific problems or enhance functionality. Methodological differences include qualitative methods, quantitative methods, and technical methodologies.

Educational approaches and curricula vary, with arts focusing on hands-on practice, creative projects, and theoretical study, while sciences focus on laboratory work, experimentation, and theoretical knowledge. Technology education includes technical skills development, project-based learning, and applied problem-solving.

Resource allocation and funding vary, with arts often relying on grants, donations, and public support, while sciences receive significant funding from government agencies, research institutions, and private industry. Career paths and outcomes vary, with arts often involving freelance or project-based roles, sciences involving research, teaching, or applied work, and technology focusing on technical skills and innovation.

The academic divide between arts, sciences, and technology is a significant issue that can have negative impacts on individuals and broader societal and educational systems. It hinders interdisciplinary collaboration, limits innovation, and perpetuates inequalities. The main consequences include limited interdisciplinary innovation, missed opportunities, inequitable resource allocation, reduced educational flexibility, career path constraints, reinforced social inequality, inhibited critical and creative thinking, inefficient use of resources, and impact on personal and professional development.

A strict divide between these fields can prevent the cross-pollination of ideas, leading to missed opportunities and potential breakthroughs. Additionally, disparities in funding and resources between these fields can exacerbate existing inequalities, such as underfunding for arts education and research. Limited access to cutting-edge tools and technologies can also affect the quality of work and learning opportunities available to students and professionals. Reduced educational flexibility can result from narrowed skill sets and a lack of holistic education. Students trained in one discipline may find it challenging to transition to careers in other fields, leading to underutilization of skills. Access gaps and educational inequities can reinforce social and economic inequalities. Siloed thinking can limit creative approaches to problem-solving and reduce problem-solving capacity. Inefficient use of resources can result from duplication of efforts across fields, leading to missed synergies. Personal and professional development can be affected by a limited perspective and reduced skill diversification.

To address these negative impacts, educational institutions and organizations should promote interdisciplinary programs, improve resource allocation, encourage flexibility, and facilitate collaboration. By addressing the academic divide and promoting a more integrated approach, we can enhance educational outcomes, drive innovation, and create a more inclusive and effective academic environment. To challenge the academic/ learning divide, there are several strategies to promote interdisciplinary collaboration, such as integrating arts, sciences, and technology, reforming educational approaches, enhancing resource sharing, offering skill development training, and encouraging diverse career pathways that combine elements of these fields. Digital humanities is one of these academic developments.

Digital Divide

The Digital Divide defines the disparity in access to digital technologies and the internet among different student groups, influenced by factors like income level, geographic location, and infrastructure availability, affecting online learning and accessing digital resources.

Socio-Economic Divide

The socio-economic divide denotes the disparities in educational outcomes and opportunities based on factors such as family income, parental education, and access to educational support, which can significantly impact students' academic performance.

Geographic and Locational Divide

Geographic and locational divide reflects variations in educational quality and resources based on students' location, influenced by factors like urban vs. rural settings, regional funding disparities, and local educational policies, resulting in challenges like fewer resources and limited extracurricular opportunities.

Cultural and Linguistic Divide

Cultural and linguistic differences in education can lead to educational experiences and outcomes for non-native speakers or diverse students, requiring additional support for success.

Disability Divide

The Disability Divide is also a learning divide which represents disparities in educational access and outcomes for students with disabilities, influenced by factors like accommodations, specialized resources, and inclusive teaching practices.

Addressing Learning Divides

Equitable Resource Allocation

The goal is to ensure equitable distribution of educational resources, including technology, textbooks, and teaching materials, and support initiatives supporting underfunded schools and communities.

Enhanced Access to Technology

Implement programs to provide technology grants, subsidies, or loaner devices to disadvantaged students to expand access to digital devices and internet connectivity.

Targeted Support Programs

Implement targeted support programs like tutoring, mentorship, and after-school activities for students from diverse backgrounds, while also providing additional language support and culturally relevant teaching materials for non-native language students.

Professional Development for Educators

The Professional Development for Educators program provides training and resources to help educators understand and address the needs of diverse students, including those with disabilities and socio-economic or cultural groups, promoting inclusive teaching practices and differentiated instruction.

Policy and Advocacy

Advocate for educational policies that promote equity and reduce disparities, supporting initiatives to reduce inequalities and enhance access to high-quality education for all students.

Conclusion

Learning divides in academics highlight the disparities in educational opportunities and outcomes among different groups of students. Addressing these divides requires a multi-faceted approach that includes equitable resource allocation, improved access to technology, targeted support programs, professional development for educators, and supportive policies. By tackling these divides, we can work towards creating a more equitable educational system that provides all students with the opportunity to succeed and reach their full potential.

Works Cited and Recommended Readings

David Michael Berry. Understanding Digital Humanities. Basingstoke, Palgrave Macmillan, 2012.

Edward Osborne Wilson. Consilience: The Unity of Knowledge. Abacus, 2010.

Snow, C. P. The Two Cultures and the Scientific Revolution; the Rede Lecture, 1959. University Press, 1962.

Gold, Matthew K. Debates in the Digital Humanities. Univ Of Minnesota Press, 2012.

Schreibman, Susan, et al. A New Companion to Digital Humanities. Wiley Blackwell. Copyright, 2016.

CHAPTER THREE

TEACHING HISTORY OF DIGITAL HUMANITIES

Simple mantra: Read and practise history in DH. If you know history, you can create a better today. Teaching history of Digital Humanities is a very valuable act. I prescribeRoberto A Busa's "Perspective on Digital Humanities"(Schreibman et al.) to explore the initial history of DH. As said earlier Digital humanities, originating from humanities computing, is a field that integrates digitized and born-digital materials, merging traditional humanities disciplines with computational tools and digital publishing. It includes subjects like curation of online collections of primary sources, analysis of cultural datasets, and the use of digital philology or computational philology. The field is characterized by its emphasis on data analysis, utilizing digital editing, computational linguistics, and natural language processing. The Digital Humanities Stack, a collection of tools and technologies used in the field, is a key concept in reimagining digital humanities. Digital philologists use digital practices and technologies, such as optical character recognition, to create and analyze digital versions of objects or artefacts, adapting the field to the digital age. Roberto A. Busa's "Perspectives on Digital Humanities" narrates the examples of IBM's roles in the history of digital humanities: Index Thomisticus in making, Nature, concept and scope of digital humanities: emerging domains, Methodologies: Teaching Project-Based Texts, Key concepts of "humanities", difference between "Humanities computing," and "Digital humanities", and developments of textual informatics, cultural informatics, hermeneutic informatics through what he called "technological miniaturization."(Schreibman et al.)

The Digital Humanities has evolved significantly over the years, from early computational experiments to a vibrant field that integrates technology and humanistic inquiry. It has seen the development of digital libraries, the launch of the Digital Library Federation, and the rise of the Digital Public Library of America. The field continues to expand, offering new methods for scholarship and fostering collaboration across disciplines. The comprehension of digital environments necessitates an awareness of the fundamental aspects of digitization, such as the nature of binary code, digital file formats, the conversion of analogue materials, and the characteristics of materials that originate in digital form. It is important to recognize that all actions of digitalization inherently include the process of remediation. The interconnected circumstances of interaction serve as a significant factor in the advancement of digital humanities and other digital undertakings. The technical infrastructure is significantly shaped by the standards and practices that are developed by communities, which in turn reflect cultural values. There exist prevalent misconceptions regarding the digital world, namely the belief that it is inherently stable and archival, implying permanence. Additionally, another common fallacy is the perception of the digital realm as immaterial, detached from its analogue counterpart. Each empirical interaction with digital technology provides evidence to the contrary. (Maniar)

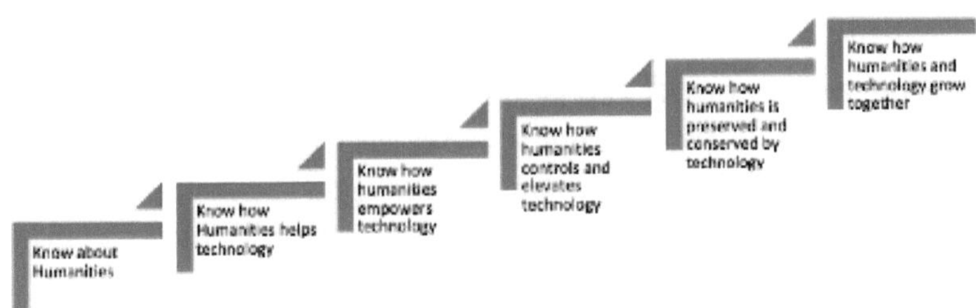

Figure 1: Technology Intersects Humanities

The foundation of all digital activity at the electrical circuit level is binary code. However, the functionality of digital environments relies on the capacity of this code to represent and process various symbolic systems.

Put simply, computing derives its power not from code as mere sequences of 1's and 0's, but rather from code's ability to encapsulate commands and information. Computation possesses far more computational capabilities compared to calculation, which primarily involves elementary mathematical operations regardless of their complexity or sophistication.

Challenges

Digital Humanities (DH) teaching presents several challenges due to its interdisciplinary nature, rapid technological advancements, and the need to balance technical skills with theoretical understanding. The field's diverse origins and diverse perspectives make it difficult to present a cohesive historical narrative. Curriculum integration is crucial for integrating DH into broader academic and technological trends, but it can be complex due to fragmented knowledge and balancing depth and breadth. Real-time technological advancements also pose challenges, as curriculum content can quickly become outdated, leading to potential gaps in the historical understanding of the field. Technological literacy is essential for students and educators to stay current with new technologies that shape DH. The emerging field of DH lacks a well-established canon of texts, milestones, or figures that can be universally agreed upon. This lack of a canonical history can lead to subjective interpretations and incomplete histories. Balancing theory and practice is essential, as students need to grasp both historical context and current technological practices. Effective teaching methods for teaching the history of DH can be challenging due to the interdisciplinary nature of the field. Engaging students with the historical aspects while also addressing contemporary issues and technologies can be difficult. Limited resources and student backgrounds may also pose challenges, making it difficult to develop comprehensive course materials. Resource and access challenges include access to archives, funding, and support. Limited access to historical digital artefacts and archives can hinder the depth and richness of historical instruction while funding limitations can impact the quality of education. Cultural and global perspectives also pose challenges. Digital Humanities has developed differently in various global contexts, and incorporating these diverse perspectives into a unified historical narrative can be challenging. Cultural biases may occur, potentially overlooking significant global developments in DH. Inclusivity and contextualization are essential for providing a comprehensive understanding of DH's evolution in different regions and cultures.

Addressing the Challenges

To address these challenges, educators can:

- Develop Interdisciplinary Curricula: Create curricula that integrate perspectives from various disciplines while providing a coherent historical narrative.
- Update Regularly: Continuously update course materials to reflect the latest technological advancements and scholarly research.
- Use Diverse Resources: Incorporate a variety of resources, including primary sources, case studies, and global perspectives, to provide a well-rounded historical account.
- Balance Theory and Practice: Ensure that students gain both theoretical knowledge and practical skills related to the history of DH.
- Innovate Pedagogical Strategies: Experiment with different teaching methods and tools to engage students and enhance their understanding of the historical development of DH.

By addressing these challenges, educators can create a more robust and engaging curriculum for teaching the history of Digital Humanities, ultimately fostering a deeper understanding of the field's evolution and impact.

The process of computation entails the manipulation of symbols using their representation in binary code. The potentialities are boundless. The advantages of encoding information, knowledge, artefacts, and other materials in a digital format are constantly weighed against the drawbacks, such as the potential loss of information from an analogue item or the vulnerability of a born-digital artefact to migration and upgrade issues. Some project details are being given to let beginners understand the basics:

Activities

1. Read "Foreword: Prospective on Digital Humanities," and present a comprehensive PPT.

2. Manually find technical terms of Roberto A. Busa used in the article, "Foreword: Prospective on Digital Humanities."

List digital humanities projects

Familiarize a list of digital humanities projects of various kinds throughout the course:

- Thomisticus Indexica: Roberto A. Busa's archival work is the beginning of computational humanities (an early form of digital humanities)
- Projects: Republic of Letters, London, Darwin's Library, Newton, Salem, NYPL, Quixote
- Walt Whitman Archive: http://www.whitmanarchive.org/
- Roman Forum Project: http://dlib.etc.ucla.edu/projects/Forum
- Women Writers Project: http://www.wwp.brown.edu/
- Encyclopaedia of Chicago: http://www.encyclopedia.chicagohistory.org/
- Computer History Museum: http://commons.gc.cuny.edu/wiki/index.php/Sample_Projects http://digitalhumanitiesnow.org/category/featured/page/10/

Some web links for Digital Humanities concepts may be familiarized

- Turing machines: <http://plato.stanford.edu/entries/turing-machine/>
- Turning machine simulator>: <http://morphett.info/turing/turing.html>
- Binary code: <http://www.theproblemsite.com/codes/binary.asp>
- History of computing: <http://www.computerhistory.org/timeline/>

Phases of DH Development

Phase 1: Foundational Growth

The field of digital humanities has its roots in the pioneering work of Roberto Busa in 1946. The TEI project, launched in 1987, led to the publication of the first full version of the TEI Guidelines in 1994. The Stanford Encyclopedia of Philosophy was initiated in 1995 and is a dynamic reference work maintained by scholars.

Phase 2: Institutional growth

Institutional growth in digital humanities includes the launch of the first specialized journal, Computers and the Humanities, in 1966. The Computer Applications and Quantitative Methods in Archaeology (CAA) association was founded in 1973, followed by the Association for Literary and Linguistic Computing (ALLC) and the Association for Computers and the Humanities (ACH) in 1978. The Alliance of Digital Humanities Organizations (ADHO) is a vital organization in the Digital Humanities field, established in 2005 at the University of Illinois, Urbana-Champaign. Its mission is to promote collaboration, communication, and the integration of digital tools and methodologies in humanities research. ADHO connects communities across disciplines and geographical boundaries, offering a platform for sharing knowledge and best practices. It organizes the annual Digital Humanities conference, which showcases research, methodologies, and networking. ADHO supports various digital humanities journals, promoting open access to scholarly work and enhancing research visibility. ADHO advocates for the recognition and integration of Digital Humanities within academia and public discourse, engaging in discussions about policies affecting digital scholarship. ADHO provides training and resources to scholars and practitioners, including mentorship opportunities for emerging scholars. It emphasizes diversity and inclusion, creating an equitable environment for all participants and encouraging participation from a global community. The National Endowment for the Humanities (NEH) launched the Digital Humanities Initiative in 2006, renamed the Office of Digital Humanities in 2008.

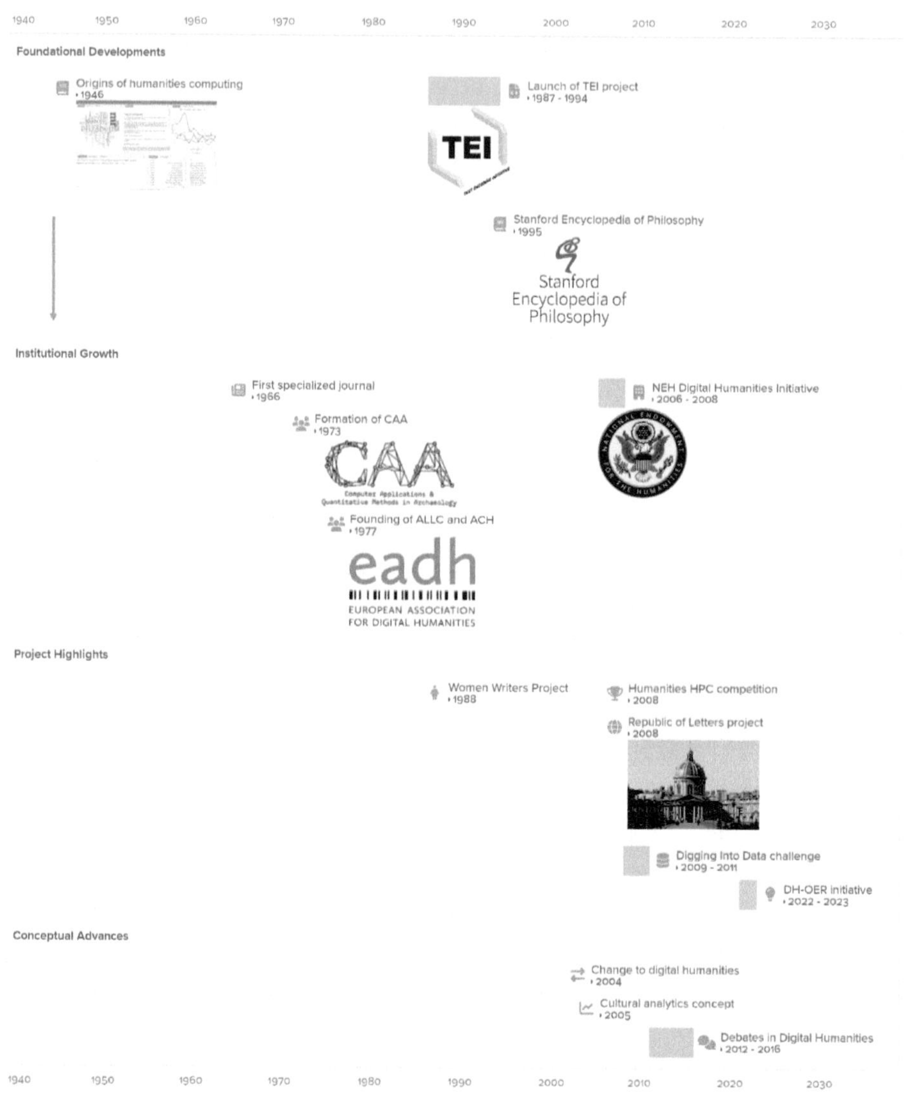

Figure 2: A Visual Timeline of Development of Digital Humanities

As an active member of ADHO, I observed that the Alliance of Digital Humanities Organizations (ADHO) is a key organization in the field of Digital Humanities, promoting collaboration, communication, and advocacy. It organizes annual conferences, supports digital humanities journals, advocates for digital scholarship, provides professional development opportunities, and promotes diversity and inclusion. ADHO encourages global engagement and inclusivity in the field.

Phase 3: Project highlights

Project highlights include the Women Writers Project, which began in 1988 to make pre-Victorian women writers more accessible through an electronic collection. The Humanities High Performance Computing competition was sponsored by the NEH Office of Digital Humanities in 2008, showcasing innovative digital projects. The Republic of Letters project visualizes the social network of Enlightenment writers.

Phase 4: Conceptual advances

Conceptual advances in digital humanities include the term 'digital humanities' popularized by John Unsworth, Susan Schreibman, and Ray Siemens in 2004. Lev Manovich developed the concept of cultural analytics in 2005 and established a lab for its application in 2007. *Debates in Digital Humanities* highlighted pedagogy as a neglected aspect of the field in 2012 and 2016 editions. Valiur Rahaman's *Introducing Digital Humanities,* the first book on Digital Humanities, directed DH readers to know global developments and India in DH activities.

These phases witnessed the following events:

1940s-1960s: Early Beginnings

1949: The first use of computers in humanities research begins with the development of text analysis and the use of punch cards.

1960: The publication of "The Automated Humanities" discusses early applications of computing in the humanities.

1970s: Foundations and Early Projects

1971: Project Gutenberg is founded, making literary works available in digital format, one of the earliest large-scale digitization efforts.

1979: The Text Encoding Initiative (TEI) is established to create guidelines for encoding literary and linguistic texts in digital formats.

1980s: Expanding Tools and Methods

1982: The first digital humanities conference, "Humanities and the Computer," takes place, bringing together scholars interested in digital methods.

1987: The Association for Computers and the Humanities (ACH) is founded, promoting the application of computing in humanities research.

1990s: Growth and Institutionalization

1990: The launch of the "Humanities Computing Yearbook" highlights ongoing projects and developments in the field.

1993: The first issue of "Digital Scholarship in the Humanities" (formerly known as "Literary and Linguistic Computing") is published.

1997: The Modern Language Association (MLA) establishes a committee on the digital humanities, recognizing its importance in academic discourse.

2000s: Mainstream Adoption and Innovation

2000: The launch of the Digital Library Federation, promoting the development of digital libraries and access to cultural heritage materials.

2004: The "Digital Humanities" term gains prominence, with the first Digital Humanities conference held in Urbana-Champaign.

2006: The Alliance of Digital Humanities Organizations (ADHO) is formed to foster collaboration among various digital humanities organizations.

2010s: Global Expansion and Collaboration

2010: The Digital Public Library of America (DPLA) is launched, providing access to a wealth of digitized cultural heritage materials.

2013: The term "Digital Humanities" is further established in academia, with many universities offering specialized programs and courses.

2014: The "DH 2014" conference in Lausanne, Switzerland, showcases the growing diversity of digital humanities projects and methodologies.

2020s: Maturity and Integration

2020: The COVID-19 pandemic accelerates the adoption of digital tools in humanities scholarship, with virtual conferences and online collaboration becoming commonplace.

2021: Increased focus on data ethics, digital equity, and inclusion in digital humanities projects.

2023: Continued evolution of tools, methodologies, and interdisciplinary collaboration, with a growing emphasis on AI and machine learning in humanities research.

Emerging Voices 2020 Onwards: Postcolonials and Digital Humanities in India

Since 2020, postcolonial studies and Digital Humanities (DH) in India have converged, with new platforms like digital archives and online exhibitions allowing for broader access and analysis. Scholars are applying postcolonial theory to DH, challenging global narratives and advocating for local contexts. Interdisciplinary collaborations, multilingual digital content, and public scholarship are also gaining attention. This evolution enriches the field of Digital Humanities and deepens our understanding of postcolonial narratives. With publication of two works Valiur Rahaman's *Introducing Digital Humanities* (2016 first book by an Indian author and publisher for Indian non-engineering background learners available at low cost), and Roopika Risam's *New Digital Worlds: Postcolonial Digital Humanities in Theory, Praxis, and Pedagogy* (2018) the idea of culture in digitals could explore further. Rahaman argues for the need of challenging mispresentations through DH learning. Ania Loomba, Matthew K. Gold, Raúl Romero, Ruth Frith, Katherine Bode, Madhusree Dutta, Diana P. Kim, Ravi Sundaram, Janelle Joseph, Shobhana Xavier, and Ishita Banerjee-Dube are other scholars in postcolonial DH studies, focusing on the intersections of colonialism, race, gender, digital tools, and cultural representation. Rupika's Digital humanities aim for openness and democratization, and raises inequalities in race, gender, sexuality, disability, and nation. Postcolonial digital humanities, for her, can address these inequalities by decentering global organizations and examining human futures in digital worlds.

Attainment of Outcomes

Teaching Digital Humanities (DH) involves achieving several educational goals to enhance students' understanding of the field's evolution, methodologies, and impact on scholarship and society. These outcomes include understanding historical development, critical analysis of methodologies, appreciation of interdisciplinary contributions, awareness of technological impact, development of research skills, integration of ethical and cultural perspectives, and enhanced communication skills. By presenting a chronological approach, using case studies and guest lectures, students gain contextual knowledge and historical insight. They also develop methodological awareness, analytical skills, and a holistic understanding of DH's contributions from various fields. By integrating ethical and cultural perspectives, students gain a deeper understanding of DH's implications and prepare them for future research and professional work in DH.

Works Cited and Recommended Readings

Alan Liu, "The State of the Digital Humanities" <http://liu.english.ucsb.edu/the-state-of-the-digital-humanities-a-report-and-a- critique/ http://liu.english.ucsb.edu/the-meaning-of-the-digital-humanities/>

Berry, D. "The Computational Turn," Introduction <www.culturemachine.net/index.php/cm/article/.../440/470>

Jones, Steven E. The Emergence of the Digital Humanities. Routledge, 2013.

Michael Kramer, "What Does Digital Humanities Bring to the Table?" <http://www.michaeljkramer.net/issuesindigitalhistory/blog/?p=862>

Rahaman, Valiur. *Introducing Digital Humanities.* Jaipur: RSBA, 2016. Available at <https://www.amazon.in/Introducing-Digital-Humanities/dp/9385528327>

Roberto A. Busa, "Perspectives of Digital Humanities" <https://companions.digitalhumanities.org/DH/?chapter=content/9781405103213_contributors.html>

Schreibman, Susan, et al. A New Companion to Digital Humanities. Wiley Blackwell. Copyright, 2016.

CHAPTER FOUR

Teaching Digital Humanities Projects, Platforms, and Tools

Teach to provoke, motivate and inspire them to become project masters. I prescribe Dubrovina, L. et al "Digital humanitarian project as a component of digital humanities" for Teaching Digital Humanities (DH) projects, platforms, and tools. They involve equipping students with both theoretical knowledge and practical skills. DH combines traditional humanities disciplines with digital tools and methods to analyze, interpret, and present humanistic data in innovative ways. This chapter explores strategies for teaching these aspects effectively, ensuring that students can engage with DH projects and utilize platforms and tools proficiently.

1. Understanding Digital Humanities Projects: Introduce students to various types of DH projects and their methodologies, including text analysis, digital editions, data visualization, digital archives, and spatial humanities.
2. Introducing Digital Humanities Platforms: Familiarize students with platforms commonly used in digital humanities research and projects, such as Omeka, Scalar, and WordPress.
3. Exploring Digital Humanities Tools: Teach students how to use digital tools for analyzing, visualizing, and presenting data in humanities research.

4. Developing Digital Humanities Skills: Equip students with the skills necessary to manage and contribute to DH projects effectively.
5. Assessing Digital Humanities Work: Develop methods for evaluating the effectiveness and quality of DH projects and student work.

Key Concepts include assessment criteria, feedback mechanisms, rubrics, peer review processes, and showcase events. By providing students with knowledge of various DH projects, familiarizing them with platforms and tools, and developing their technical and critical skills, educators can prepare them to contribute effectively to the field of digital humanities. This chapter aims to provide a framework for teaching these components in an engaging, informative, and aligned manner with the evolving needs of the discipline.

Introduction

The chapter presents teaching the analysis of Digital Humanities, Projects, Platforms, and Tools. Every digital project shares common structural characteristics. Some systems used in the digital humanities field are either purpose-built inside the community (e.g., ORANGE, Atlas.ti, Omeka, the like platform learners will use for their projects), repurposed software (e.g., WordPress, Drupal), or custom-made. When discussing digital projects, we refer to the "back end" and "front end", which respectively encompass the technical aspects such as server files, browser files, databases, search engines, processing programs, and networks, as well as the user experience. Since the presentation of digital information on a screen is defined by HTML (hypertext markup language), all digital projects must be generated in HTML as their ultimate format. However, what is responsible for generating the user experience on the backend? How are digital projects organised to facilitate diverse user tasks and activities?(Chansanam et al.; Berry and Fagerjord; Dubrovina et al.) Every digital humanities project consists of fundamental structural elements, however, the level of intricacy that can be included in these elements and their interconnections with each other and the user might grow tremendously. The essential components are a collection of data or digital resources, a well-organized information framework, a set of functionalities, and a user interface for optimal user interaction. Although seemingly uncomplicated and oversimplified, this approach proves valuable for conceptualising the development of digital humanities projects. At their most basic level, digital projects can be a collection of files (assets) kept in an organised system of information such as a database or file system (structure), from which they can be retrieved (services) and displayed by a web browser (use/display).

Exercise 1

Explain the values and basic elements of the projects.

The complexity in digital humanities projects arises from the various methods we employ to establish a structure (i.e., incorporating information into the fundamental data) in the assets, arrange the information architecture or structure, and so provide intricate services accessed through the display. The clarity of the information will improve as we progress into the examination of specific instances. Despite its simplicity or even its rudimentary nature, this picture illustrates the fundamental framework of all digital humanities projects. Please note that the server, network, and other system requirements are not included in this context. Learners must know about DH projects, the nature of projects, their relevance and feasibility and their power to be monetized in future. Hence, the teacher provides a list of digital humanities works, for example, Pelagios etc. Here some lists are given as teaching tools for DH students. Students are open viewers, visitors, and rompers of many sites in a day. They are of no use. Let's drive them to the most useful knowledge-based sites. And, let them know about them.

"Pelagios" ™

"PELAGIOS"™ is an acronym for 'Pelagios: Enable Linked Ancient Geodata In Open Systems'. Its purpose is to facilitate the integration of Linked Open Data into online platforms that make reference to locations in the Ancient World. What is the rationale behind our desire to pursue that action? It enables various other possibilities, such as novel methods of exploration and representation for academics and the general population. Pelagios, in addition to its literal meaning of 'of the sea', symbolises the extensive network of maritime routes that served as the main communication channels in the ancient world. We find this metaphor fitting for a digital tool that aims to link mentions of ancient locations. Let students know about its alliances. It is a global alliance of projects and research groups:

Sr. No.	Project Titles	Host Institutes
1.	"Google Ancient Places"	Open University, University of Southampton
2.	"LUCERO"	The Open University
3.	"Pleiades"	Institute for the Study of the Ancient World, NYU
4.	"Perseus Digital Library"	Tufts University
5.	"Arachne"	University of Cologne
6.	"SPQR"	King's College, London
7.	"Digital Memory Engineering"	Austrian Institute of Technology)
8.	"Open Context"	UC Berkeley
9.	"nomisma.org"	American Numismatic Society
10.	"PtolemyMachine"	College of the Holy Cross
11.	"CLAROS"	University of Oxford

Table 1: Completed DH Projects at Various Institutes

1. Pelagios: <https://pelagios.org/>

It consolidates digital humanities projects into a unified portal, involving scholars, scientists, and curators using linked data methodologies to explore historical phenomena, observing their organization and arrangement. http://pelagios-project.blogspot.com/

Class-Activities

Ask students to perform the following tasks in class.

a. Understand the site? Go through the links/resources.
b. Roam through the Tabs, widgets, and menus.
c. Understand "Perspectives on Digital Humanities"
d. Compare and contrast a "website" with a digital humanities project. Which dimensions distinguish Pelagios?

e. Analyse these instances and define their structure using the essential components described above Consider community, scholarship, digital infrastructure, values in the languages, practises, and organisation of the component sections as you work through this complex project.

Teaching Virtual /e-Projects

Students may be assigned the following software and represent results with PPTs.

1. **"Arachne"**™ Why Arachne is? How does it work? Process and Flow-works
2. **"British Museum"** Think about how it was created and why. What is its value in today's scenario?
3. **"CLAROS"**™ How does it begin with what objectives? Are they still attaining those objectives?
4. **"FASTI"** <https://www.fastionline.org/> Who are the developers of this site? What is the major domain of this platform?
5. **"Google Ancient Places"** Give at least 1 hour daily to understand how it works.
6. **"Inscriptions of Israel/Palestine"** <https://www.inscriptionsisraelpalestine.org>What is digital conservation? How it was made? Who sponsored?
7. **"ISAWPapers"** <https://isaw.nyu.edu/publications/isaw-papers> Discuss subjects of this platform.
8. **"LUCERO"** Get involved on this platform.
9. **"Meketre"** Why it is a network of knowledge?
10. **"Nomisma"** How coins are cultural artefacts? Should they be conserved?
11. **"OCRE"** What are its aims? Can you devise any such aims for developing a system?
12. **"Open Context"** Understand the web work and project funds.
13. **"ORACC"** trace its objectives.
14. **"Papyri.Info"** Evaluate the project for its service to provide knowledge.
15. **"Perseus Digital Library"** Myth is the preservable domain. Why?
16. **"Ports Antiques"**: Get the subject matters that have made the site valuable.

17. **“Ptolemy machine”**: Why the project is incomprehensible to you?
18. **“Regnum Francorum”** Why any such projects should be funded?
19. **“SPQR”**: Extrapolate the European Aggregator and make your blog to post it.
20. **“SquinchPix”** Make your blog and try posting facts as you find here

Why are these sites not included on Pelagius?

1. <http://isaw.nyu.edu//ancient-world-image-bank>
2. <http://www.inscriptifact.com/>
3. <http://isaw.nyu.edu/ancient-world-image-bank>

Attainment of Outcomes

This chapter focused on the back end of digital humanities projects, focusing on the combination of digital assets, services, and user experience, and how students will get ideas on designing proposals for DH research projects. The field of "digital humanities" combines the methodologies of humanities and engineering sciences to enhance their potential through effective interaction in the context of digitalization and innovation. An integral component of the digital humanities infrastructure involves doing research initiatives aimed at generating resources and databases that encompass humanities knowledge.

CHAPTER FIVE

Teaching Markup and Hyper Text Marking Language

Teaching HTML effectively leads to key outcomes for learners, including mastery of basic syntax and structure, the ability to create structured web pages, and the ability to organize content, insert images, and implement forms. Let us see if it is possible to teach HTML the non-engineering/coding/mathematical students.

Introduction

Teaching HyperText Markup Language (HTML) effectively includes a combination of clear explanations, practical examples, theoretical concepts and hands-on experience. HTML is a fundamental knowledge of technology for developing web pages and comprehending it is essential for anyone interested in web development. The chapter briefly explains the value of teaching HTML to non-mathematical, technology students. The Web with HTML was invented by Tim Berners-Lee at CERN (*Consell European pour la Researche Nucleaire*). It is often used to develop websites. It is not programming but a mark-up language. The HTML is comprised of four tags HTML, title, head, and body. The HTML tags are written by using open tags (< >) and closed tags (</>). It is divided into three categories: transitional, strict, and frameset.

Teaching the basics of HTML (HyperText Markup Language) involves introducing students to the fundamental concepts and elements used to create web pages. Here's a structured approach to teaching HTML fundamentals, including objectives, key topics, and practical exercises:

Teaching Introduction to HTML

Fix an Objective: To understand what HTML is, its role in web development, and its basic structure.

1. Definition: Explain HTML as a markup language used to structure content on the web.
2. History and Evolution: Brief overview of HTML's evolution from HTML 1.0 to HTML5.
3. Document Structure: Introduction to the basic structure of an HTML document.

I outline some key aspects to consider when teaching HTML to non-engineering background students of humanities and social sciences:

1. Understanding the Basics: Definition and Purpose

- Teaching HTML effectively includes using real-world examples, encouraging experimentation, providing constructive feedback, and fostering collaboration to build teamwork and problem-solving skills.
- Begin with explaining what HTML is, and how a markup language is used to structure content on the web. Emphasize its role in defining elements like headings, paragraphs, links, and images.
- Basic Structure: Teach the basic structure of an HTML document, including the <!DOCTYPE html>, <html>, <head>, and <body> tags. Make sure students understand the purpose of each part.

2. Core HTML Elements:

- Text Formatting: Cover essential tags such as <h1> to <h6>, <p>, <strong>, <em>, and <br>. Explain how these tags affect the appearance and structure of text.

- Links and Images: Show how to use <a> for hyperlinks and <img> for images, including attributes like href and src.
- Lists and Tables: Teach how to create ordered (<ol>) and unordered lists (<ul>), as well as tables (<table>, <tr>, <td>, <th>).

3. Hands-On Practice

- Interactive Exercises: Use interactive exercises and coding challenges to reinforce learning. Have students create simple web pages to apply what they've learned.
- Projects: Assign projects that require students to build complete web pages or small websites. This helps them understand how different HTML elements work together in a real-world context.

4. Modern HTML and Best Practices

- HTML5 Features: Introduce HTML5 elements like <header>, <footer>, <section>, and <article>, which offer semantic meaning and better organization of content.
- Accessibility and Semantics: Teach the importance of writing semantic HTML for accessibility and search engine optimization (SEO). Explain how proper use of tags can enhance web accessibility for people with disabilities.

5. Integration with Other Technologies

- CSS and JavaScript: Show how HTML interacts with CSS (for styling) and JavaScript (for interactivity). Basic integration examples can help students see the broader context of web development.
- Web Development Tools: Introduce students to web development tools such as text editors (e.g., VS Code), browsers‘ developer tools, and version control systems like Git.

6. Teaching Methods and Resources

Visual Aids

Use diagrams and visual aids to illustrate HTML structures and the impact of various tags on web page layout.

Code Examples

Provide plenty of code examples and templates for students to study and modify.

Feedback and Assessment

- Offer regular feedback on student projects and assignments to help them improve their skills.
- Assess their understanding through quizzes and practical exercises.

7. Staying Updated

- Ensure that the content you teach reflects the latest HTML standards and best practices. HTML evolves, and keeping up with changes can be beneficial for students.
- Encourage students to explore online resources, communities, and documentation for further learning and support.

Offering Challenges and Solutions

Keeping Students Engaged

HTML can be quite straightforward, but maintaining engagement might require integrating practical and creative tasks to keep students interested.

Ensuring Comprehension

- Ensure that all students understand the foundational concepts before moving on to more advanced topics.
- Use assessments to gauge their grasp of HTML basics.

By understanding these aspects, you can effectively teach HTML and provide students with the skills needed to create and understand web content. Emphasizing practical applications and modern best practices will help students build a strong foundation for further learning in web development.

HTML in Learning Humanities

HTML is a powerful tool in the humanities for creating digital projects, organizing information, and presenting research in innovative ways. Examples include creating digital exhibits, building interactive timelines, developing digital text analysis tools, creating interactive literature maps, designing online book reviews or critiques, and building interactive bibliographies. By integrating HTML with other technologies like CSS and JavaScript, students and educators can explore new ways of presenting and analyzing humanities content. The chapter defines the ways to teach the basics of HTML, the function of Structured Data, Content Modelling, Interpretation, and Display.

All data in digital formats can be categorised as either structured or unstructured. Actuality, all data is systematically arranged—even when inputting on a keyboard, it arranges a text as an alphabetical file and associates it with an ASCII keyboard and keystrokes. The distinction between individual letters or numbers is what arranges the data at its most basic level. However, the phrase "structured data" refers to an extra level of organisation that allows for the management and manipulation of data using this additional structure. Common techniques for arranging data are using tags for markup, utilising comma-separated values, or employing alternative data structures. The distinction between organised and unstructured data has ramifications for the approaches via which information can be exploited, analysed, and displayed. The secondary levels of organisation, referred to as encoding, outlined previously, impart clear formal characteristics to structured data. These utilise additional elements (such as tags, which will be explained in more detail), data structures (tables, spreadsheets, databases), or alternative approaches to enrich the data by offering an extra level of interpretation or value. Unstructured data refers to words, photographs, music files, or other digitally encoded information that does not have a predetermined organisational structure.

Exemplary Illustration

Let's examine the literary material of the play *Romeo and Juliet*, prescribed in the university curriculum. The lines in the play are arranged in alphabetical order. Nevertheless, the text is additionally divided into lines spoken by the characters, stage directions, and information about the act, scene, and other pertinent features. To identify any instance of the name "Juliet," a simple string search can be employed. This is an investigation of disorganised data. However, to obtain all the lines said by Juliet, it is important to include a tag, such as <proper_name>, within the text. The degree of detail enforced by the structure will determine the level of control we have over the manipulation and/or analysis. Every line can be assigned properties such as class, race, and gender. Nevertheless, if our objective is to classify and scrutinise all the lines that include offensive language, this specific assemblage of tags or structures would prove to be ineffectual. Every act of organising results in an additional level of analysis and is, in itself, an act of analysis that has important implications.

Other Markup Languages

There are various types of markup languages available. HTML, XML, XHTML, SGML, LaTeX, RTF, YAML, CSS, and TEI are unavoidable markup languages. Markup languages are essential in computing for defining and formatting documents, especially on the web. HTML is the standard markup language used for web page creation, XML for data storage and transport, XHTML for XML-compliant document structure, SGML for defining generalized markup languages, LaTeX for typesetting documents, Markdown for plain text formatting, RTF for text formatting and document layout, YAML for human-readable data serialization format, CSS for controlling the presentation of web documents, and TEI is used in text0based initiatives to Digital Humanities. Each markup language serves different purposes and is suited to various contexts, making it crucial to understand these different types to select the right tool for multiple tasks in computing and digital content creation. Further, you ought to speak to the students about the values, functions, and utility of markup languages.

XML (eXtensible Markup Language)

Purpose: XML is used to store and transport data. It is both human-readable and machine-readable, making it ideal for data interchange.

Key Features

- Custom Tags: Users define their tags to structure data.
- Hierarchy: Data is organized hierarchically with nested tags.
- Strict Syntax: Requires proper nesting and closing of tags

Basic codes

```
<?xml version="1.0" encoding="UTF-8"?>
    <book>
<title>XML Guide</title>
<author>Valiur</author>
<year>2024</year>
</book>
```

XHTML (eXtensible HyperText Markup Language)

Purpose: XHTML is a stricter version of HTML designed to be more XML-compliant, ensuring better document structure and compatibility.

Key Features

- XML Syntax: Follows XML syntax rules, including properly closed tags and attribute quoting.
- Document Structure: Similar to HTML but with stricter syntax rules.

Basic Codes

```
<?xml version="1.0"?>
<!DOCTYPE html PUBLIC "-//W3C//DTD XHTML 1.0 Strict//EN" "http://www.w3.org/TR/xhtml1/DTD/xhtml1-strict.dtd">
<html xmlns="http://www.w3.org/1999/xhtml">
<head>
<title>XHTML Example</title>
</head>
<body>
<h1>XHTML Page</h1>
<p>This is a paragraph in XHTML.</p>
</body>
</html>
```

SGML (Standard Generalized Markup Language)

Purpose: SGML is a standard for defining generalized markup languages. It serves as the basis for HTML and XML.

Key Features

Flexibility: Allows for the definition of custom tags and document structures.

Complexity: More complex and less user-friendly than HTML or XML.

Example Code: SGML examples are similar to XML but often more verbose and less commonly used today. It's more a framework for defining markup languages rather than a practical example of content.

LaTeX

Purpose: LaTeX is used for typesetting documents, particularly in academia, for producing technical and scientific documents with complex formatting.

Key Characteristics:

Document Preparation: Focuses on high-quality typesetting and is widely used for writing research papers, theses, and books.

Basic Commands

Uses commands like \section{}, \begin{document}, and \end{document} to structure documents.

```
\documentclass{article}
\begin{document}
\title{Introduction to LaTeX}
\author{Jane Doe}
\date{\today}
\maketitle
\section{Introduction}
This is a section in a LaTeX document.
\end{document}
```

Markdown

Purpose: Markdown is a lightweight markup language used for formatting plain text. It is often used in README files, documentation, and content management systems.

Key Characteristics:

Simplicity: Uses plain text formatting with simple syntax like # for headings and * for lists.

Conversion: Easily converted to HTML and other formats.

Basic Commands

```
# My Document
This is a paragraph in Markdown.
## Subheading
- List item 1
- List item 2
[Link to Example](https://www.example.com)
```

RTF (Rich Text Format)

Purpose: RTF is a text file format that allows for text formatting and document layout. It is used for exchanging documents between different word processors.

Key Characteristics:

Formatting: Supports text styles, fonts, and colours.

Compatibility: Ensures document compatibility across various platforms.

Basic Codes

```
{\rtf1\ansi\ansicpg1252\deff0\nouicompat\
deflang1033{\fonttbl{\f0\fnil\fcharset0 Calibri;}}
\viewkind4\uc1\pard\sa200\sl276\slmult1\f0\fs22\lang9 This is a
sample RTF document.\par
}
```

YAML (YAML Ain't Markup Language)

Purpose: YAML is a human-readable data serialization format used for configuration files and data exchange.

Key Features

Human-Readable: Uses indentation and simple syntax to structure data.

Data Serialization: Often used for configuration files and data storage.

```
book:
title: "DH Essentials"
author: "Arnold"
year: 2024
```

CSS (Cascading Style Sheets)

Purpose: Although not a markup language, CSS is used alongside HTML to control the presentation of web documents. It styles the HTML content.

Key Features

Selectors and Properties: Uses selectors to apply styles to HTML elements.

Responsive Design: Supports responsive design techniques for different devices.

Basic Code

```
body {
font-family: Arial, sans-serif;
background-color: #f0f0f0;
}
   h1 {
color: #333;
}
   p {
line-height: 1.6;
}
```

Values, Functions, and Utility of Markup Languages

HTML is the most widely utilised and renowned form of markup. Its purpose was to standardise the presentation of files sent over the internet, allowing them to be easily read by web browsers and displayed on screens. Diverse academic pursuits utilise alternate markup languages, and the fundamental principles of HTML apply to their utilisation, notwithstanding the differences in each markup language. SGML, an acronym for standardised generic markup language, was the original markup language developed for the Web. Officially, it is classified as a metalanguage, which denotes its purpose as a language employed to describe other languages. The creation of mark-up languages aimed to establish a standardised means of communication on the Internet. Their primary goal is to guarantee the uniform presentation of files across different web browsers and operating systems. Useful resources for understanding mark-up may be found at:<http://www.w3.org/MarkUp/SGML/> <http://wwwsul.stanford.edu/tools/tutorials/html2.0/gentle.html>

Geospatial information uses KML, while numerous text-based initiatives adhere to TEI, which stands for Text Encoding Initiative. These standards facilitate inter-project communication and data sharing. An effective practice is to thoroughly examine a collection of tags specific to a certain field within your area of interest or competence, and potentially create your own set of tags. For example, the development of a specialised set of tags enables individuals operating within a common knowledge area to establish uniformity across various collections of documents produced by different users (such as Golf Markup Language, Music Markup Language, Chemical Markup Language, etc.). However, a mark-up language serves as a naming system and a means to formalise the items inside a specific domain of knowledge or expressions, such as texts, scores, performances, and documents. Despite the increasing dominance of natural language processing (NLP), structured data continues to be the prevailing method for establishing standards and formal systems, and doing data analysis. Structured data is important when dealing with large, complicated collections of documents or when integrating data from different users or repositories. Data formats adhere to standards, enabling uniform search and analysis of data within files.

If, on one occasion, you annotate *Romeo and Juliet* using the <girl> and <boy> tags, and on a subsequent occasion, another person employs the <man> and <woman> tags to refer to the same characters, this results in an inconsistency. The practical use of standards is inherently challenging, as inconsistency is an inherent reality. Data crosswalks, which aim to align values between different sets of terms, only provide a partial solution to this issue. However, organising data is an essential component of Digital Humanities work. The W3C (World Wide Web Consortium) is responsible for maintaining the standards, definitions, usage norms, and recommendations for tags in markup languages. The page also includes a compilation of current markup languages, which are captivating to peruse. Visit the website: <http://www.w3.org/MarkUp/SGML/>

Value of Knowing the Sidebar and HTML

Having a grasp of the fundamental concepts of any markup language enables you to apply this understanding to any other markup language. Due to its widespread usage, HTML serves as an excellent foundation for beginners. In essence, every file presented on the Internet utilises HTML to be interpreted by a web browser. HTML serves as the fundamental language of the web, although other file types such as jpg, mp3, and png can be incorporated into HTML frameworks, similar to how physical frames hold pictures, televisions, speakers, or aquariums. The term "mark-up" language is used to describe this language since it utilises tags to provide instructions to a browser regarding the presentation of information in a file. HTML can be seen as rudimentary and simplistic. Initially, it provoked frustration among visual designers due to its utilisation of a basic set of commands to display text solely based on size and emphasis (boldness). Initially, HTML did not include any provision for the utilisation of particular fonts, for example. HTML elements are used to designate specific components within a file, such as a header, paragraph, or line break, to establish a consistent display format. Essentially, it functions as encoded directives for the browser. All markup languages and structured data must adhere to the principles of being well-formed. Consequently, the files must adhere to the principles of markup to be shown correctly or "parsed" by the browser. A file that fails to parse might be likened to a performance performed in a sport where it is out of place (such as a home run in football) or a flawed structure (like a circle that does not shut) because it does not adhere to the established rules.

HTML is a metalinguistic system that operates according to its own set of regulations as well as those of all markup languages. Markup languages facilitate data structuring, enabling their utilisation for analysis purposes. HTML tags are used to annotate the physical characteristics of publications, rather than to analyse their content. HTML lacks tags, for example, a girl named <proper_name_female_girl>. However, in a textual markup system, a more intricate method of organising information permits attributes to modify terms and tags to generate a significantly advanced level of analysis of semantic (meaning) value in a document. When markup languages are interpreted and analysed, they can be processed before displaying the information contained inside them. For example, one can retrieve all occurrences of a male speaker using offensive language. Instructions dictate the operations of data selection, transformation, and display. Display can be controlled by the use of style sheets, allowing for the application of global instructions to whole collections of documents, rather than individually styling each item.

A sidebar is a vertical column or panel that is typically displayed on one side of a web page or application interface. It serves a variety of purposes, such as providing additional navigation options, displaying related content, or offering supplementary information. Sidebars can be found on websites, blogs, applications, and content management systems, and they often enhance the user experience by organizing and presenting secondary content in a structured way.

Key Features of a Sidebar

Navigation: Often used to house navigation menus or links to important sections of a website or application. This allows users to quickly access different areas without scrolling through the main content.

Supplementary Information: Can display related articles, popular posts, advertisements, or widgets like weather forecasts or social media feeds.

Customization: Many websites and applications allow users or administrators to customize the content and layout of sidebars to better suit their needs.

Responsiveness: In modern web design, sidebars often have responsive designs. They may be hidden or collapsed into a hamburger menu on smaller screens to save space.

Examples of Sidebar Usage

Websites

Blog Sites: Sidebars might include categories, recent posts, archives, search bars, and social media links.

E-commerce Sites: Sidebars can feature product categories, filters, or promotional banners.

Applications

Email Clients: Sidebars may show folders, labels, or account information.

Dashboard Interfaces: Sidebars often include menus for different functionalities or settings.

Content Management Systems (CMS)

WordPress: Users can add widgets to the sidebar, such as text blocks, custom menus, or calendar widgets.

Examples of Sidebar Implementation in HTML/CSS

HTML Structure 1

```
<!DOCTYPE html>
<html>
<head>
<title>Sample Page with Sidebar</title>
<style>
body {
font-family: Arial, sans-serif;
}
.container {
display: flex;
}
.main-content {
flex: 3;
padding: 20px;
}
.sidebar {
flex: 1;
padding: 20px;
background-color: #f4f4f4;
}
</style>
</head>
<body>
<div class="container">
<div class="main-content">
<h1>Main Content Area</h1>
<p>This is where the main content goes.</p>
</div>
<div class="sidebar">
<h2>Sidebar</h2>
<p>Additional information or navigation can be placed here.</p>
</div>
</div>
</body>
</html>
```

HTML Structure 2: CSS Styling for a Responsive Sidebar

```
/* Base styles */
.container {
display: flex;
flex-direction: row;
}
    .sidebar {
background: #f4f4f4;
padding: 20px;
}
    /* Responsive styles */
@media (max-width: 768px) {
.container {
flex-direction: column;
}
.sidebar {
order: 1;
}
}
```

Instructions for Making Sidebars

Ask students to:

- Maintain Relevancy: Ensure the sidebar content is relevant to the main content or purpose of the page.
- Minimize Clutter: Avoid overcrowding the sidebar with too much information, which can distract from the main content.
- Design for Usability: Make sure the sidebar is easy to navigate and visually distinct from the main content area.
- Consider Mobile Design: Implement responsive design principles so that sidebars work well on different screen sizes.

Sidebars are versatile UI elements that, when used effectively, can greatly enhance the user experience by providing easy access to supplementary content and navigation options.

List of Exercises

- Style a page, then create a style sheet to govern all style features globally across a collection of pages.
- What does "HTML" identify?
- What does "HTML" not do?
- How is "Text Encoding Initiatives" different from "HTML"?
- Exercise find poems, translators, authors, prose, commentary, footnotes etc.
- Try extract, search, analyze, find, style.

Assign Some Intensive Exercises

HTML can be a powerful tool in the humanities for creating digital projects, organizing information, and presenting research in innovative ways. Here are some examples of how HTML can be applied in the study and teaching of the humanities:

1. Creating Digital Exhibits

Online Museum Exhibit

Description: Use HTML to build a digital exhibit showcasing historical artefacts, artwork, or literary works. This can include detailed descriptions, images, and interactive elements.

Key Features

HTML Elements: <img>, <p>, <h1>, <h2>, <a>, <div>.

Basic Code

```
<!DOCTYPE html>
<html>
```

```
<head>
<title>Virtual Museum Exhibit</title>
</head>
<body>
<header>
<h1>Virtual Museum Exhibit: Renaissance Art</h1>
</header>
<section>
<h2>The Birth of Venus by Sandro Botticelli</h2>
<img src="venus.jpg" alt="The Birth of Venus" width="600">
<p>This iconic painting by Sandro Botticelli depicts the goddess Venus
emerging from the sea on a shell.</p>
<a href="https://en.wikipedia.org/wiki/The_Birth_of_Venus"
target="_blank">Learn more</a>
</section>
<footer>
<p>Virtual Museum Exhibit created by [Your Name]</p>
</footer>
</body>
</html>
```

2. Building Interactive Timelines

Historical Event Timeline

Description: Use HTML to create an interactive timeline of significant historical events. Combine HTML with CSS and JavaScript for interactive features.

Key Features

HTML Elements: <div>, <span>, <p>, <ul>, <li>.

Basic Code

```
<!DOCTYPE html>
<html>
```

```
<head>
<title>Historical Timeline</title>
<style>
.timeline {
list-style-type: none;
padding: 0;
}
.timeline-item {
padding: 10px;
border-left: 2px solid black;
margin: 10px 0;
position: relative;
}
.timeline-item::before {
content: '';
position: absolute;
left: -6px;
top: 0;
width: 12px;
height: 12px;
border-radius: 50%;
background: black;
}
</style>
</head>
<body>
<header>
<h1>Important Historical Events</h1>
</header>
<section>
<ul class="timeline">
<li class="timeline-item">
<h2>Event 1: The Fall of Constantinople</h2>
<p>Year: 1453</p>
<p>Details: The capture of Constantinople by the Ottoman Empire marked
the end of the Byzantine Empire.</p>
</li>
<li class="timeline-item">
```

```
<h2>Event 2: The Declaration of Independence</h2>
<p>Year: 1776</p>
<p>Details: The American colonies declared their independence from Britain.</p>
</li>
</ul>
</section>
</body>
</html>
```

3. Developing Digital Text Analysis Tools

Literary Analysis Tool

Description: Create a web-based tool that allows users to analyze text for various literary elements, such as word frequency or sentiment analysis.

Key Characteristics

HTML Elements: <textarea>, <button>, <div>, <p>.

Basic Code

```
<!DOCTYPE html>
<html>
<head>
<title>Text Analysis Tool</title>
</head>
<body>
<header>
<h1>Literary Text Analyzer</h1>
</header>
<section>
<textarea id="textInput" rows="10" cols="50" placeholder="Paste your text here..."></textarea><br>
<button onclick="analyzeText()">Analyze</button>
<div id="result"></div>
```

```
</section>
<script>
function analyzeText() {
var text = document.getElementById('textInput').value;
var result = document.getElementById('result');
// Simple example: count the number of words
var wordCount = text.split(/\s+/).length;
result.innerHTML = '<p>Word Count: ' + wordCount + '</p>';
}
</script>
</body>
</html>
```

4. Creating Interactive Literature Maps

Literary Map of Settings

Description: Use HTML to create an interactive map showing locations mentioned in a literary work. This can be combined with JavaScript and mapping APIs.

Key Features

HTML Elements: <div>, <map>, <area>, <img>.

Basic Code

```
<!DOCTYPE html>
<html>
<head>
<title>Literary Map</title>
<style>
.map-container {
position: relative;
width: 800px;
}
.map-container img {
```

```
width: 100%;
}
.map-container .map-area {
position: absolute;
border: 2px solid red;
}
</style>
</head>
<body>
<header>
<h1>Map of Literary Settings</h1>
</header>
<section>
<div class="map-container">
<img src="literary_map.jpg" usemap="#literarymap" alt="Literary Map">
<map name="literarymap">
<area shape="rect" coords="34,44,270,350" href="#" alt="Setting 1" title="Setting 1">
<area shape="rect" coords="290,172,333,250" href="#" alt="Setting 2" title="Setting 2">
</map>
</div>
</section>
</body>
</html>
```

5. Designing Online Book Reviews or Critiques

Book Review Page

Description: Create a webpage where students can post book reviews, complete with ratings, summaries, and comments.

Key Features

HTML Elements: <form>, <input>, <textarea>, <button>, <div>.

Basic Code

```
<!DOCTYPE html>
<html>
<head>
<title>Book Reviews</title>
</head>
<body>
<header>
<h1>Book Reviews</h1>
</header>
<section>
<form action="/submit_review" method="post">
<label for="title">Book Title:</label>
<input type="text" id="title" name="title" required><br><br>
   <label for="author">Author:</label>
<input type="text" id="author" name="author" required><br><br>
   <label for="review">Review:</label><br>
<textarea id="review" name="review" rows="10" cols="50"
required></textarea><br><br>
   <label for="rating">Rating:</label>
<select id="rating" name="rating">
<option value="1">1</option>
<option value="2">2</option>
<option value="3">3</option>
<option value="4">4</option>
<option value="5">5</option>
</select><br><br>
   <button type="submit">Submit Review</button>
</form>
</section>
</body>
</html>
```

6. Building Interactive Bibliographies

Example: Annotated Bibliography

Description: Use HTML to create an annotated bibliography with links to sources, summaries, and annotations.

Key Features

HTML Elements: <dl>, <dt>, <dd>, <a>, <p>.

Basic Code

```
<!DOCTYPE html>
<html>
<head>
<title>Annotated Bibliography</title>
</head>
<body>
<header>
<h1>Annotated Bibliography</h1>
</header>
<section>
<dl>
<dt><a href="https://www.example.com" target="_blank">Example Book Title</a></dt>
<dd><p>Author: Jane Doe</p>
<p>Summary: This book explores the impact of digital technology on modern literature.</p>
<p>Annotation: Provides a comprehensive overview and is essential for understanding the intersection of technology and literature.</p>
</dd>
</dl>
</section>
</body>
</html>
```

These project examples demonstrate how HTML is used to create engaging, interactive, and educational resources in the humanities. *By integrating HTML with other technologies (like CSS and JavaScript) and applying it to real-world projects, students and educators can explore new ways of presenting and analyzing humanities content,* I guess.

Learn through the Websites

- Blake: <http://www.blakearchive.org/blake/>
- Look at Whitman: <http://www.whitmanarchive.org/>
- Analyse Rosetti: <http://www.rossettiarchive.org/index.html>
- Spatial history project: Republic of Letters<http://republicofletters.stanford.edu/case-study/voltaire-and-the-enlightenment/>
- VCDH: Valley of the Shadow <http://valley.lib.virginia.edu/VoS/choosepart.html>
- Salem Witch Trial Project: <http://etext.virginia.edu/salem/witchcraft/>

Tools for Annotation

- DiRT: https://digitalresearchtools.pbworks.com/w/page/17801672/FrontPage

Attainments of Learning Outcomes

Teaching HTML effectively yields several key attainments or outcomes for learners. I enumerate a comprehensive list of what students can achieve:

1. Mastery of Basic HTML Syntax and Structure

Outcome: Students can write and understand basic HTML documents, including the use of tags, attributes, and elements.

Skills Acquired

- Understanding and using core HTML tags (<html>, <head>, <body>, <h1>, <p>, <a>, <img>, etc.).
- Creating structured web pages with headers, paragraphs, lists, and links.
- Writing and validating HTML code to ensure it conforms to web standards.

2. Ability to Create and Format Web Pages

Outcome: Students are capable of building well-structured and styled web pages, laying the groundwork for more advanced web development.

Skills Acquired

- Organizing content into sections and using semantic HTML (<header>, <nav>, <section>, <article>, <footer>).
- Inserting and formatting images and links.
- Implementing basic forms for user input (<form>, <input>, <textarea>, <button>).

3. Understanding of HTML Document Structure and Metadata

Outcome: Students comprehend the overall structure of HTML documents and the role of metadata in web pages.

Skills Acquired

- Implementing document metadata (<title>, <meta>, <link>) to enhance page functionality and SEO.
- Using the <head> section effectively to include stylesheets, scripts, and other resources.
- Understanding the document object model (DOM) and its significance in web development.

4. Proficiency in Using HTML for Web Layouts

Outcome: Students can use HTML to create basic layouts and understand the principles of responsive design.

Skills Acquired

- Structuring pages using <div>, <span>, and layout elements like <header>, <nav>, and <footer>.

- Implementing responsive design principles through HTML, including the use of viewport meta tags.
- Understanding the basics of how HTML interacts with CSS for layout and design.

5. Knowledge of Accessibility and Web Standards

Outcome: Students are aware of accessibility practices and the importance of adhering to web standards for a more inclusive web experience.

Skills Acquired

- Using semantic HTML to improve accessibility and SEO.
- Implementing accessible features, such as alt attributes for images and ARIA (Accessible Rich Internet Applications) roles.
- Testing HTML code for cross-browser compatibility and accessibility compliance.

6. Capability to Integrate Multimedia Elements

Outcome: Students can embed and manage multimedia elements in web pages, enhancing content richness.

Skills Acquired

- Embedding audio and video elements using <audio> and <video> tags.
- Handling multimedia attributes, such as controls and sources.
- Understanding the integration of third-party content (e.g., embedding videos from platforms like YouTube).

7. Skill in Using Developer Tools and Debugging

Outcome: Students are proficient in using browser developer tools to inspect and debug HTML code.

Skills Acquired

- Utilizing browser developer tools to inspect HTML elements and understand their properties.
- Debugging and resolving common HTML issues using the console and other debugging features.
- Understanding how to use validation tools to ensure HTML code is error-free and standards-compliant.

8. Ability to Build Interactive Elements with HTML Forms

Outcome: Students know how to create and manage interactive forms for user input and data collection.

Skills Acquired

- Designing forms with various input types (<input>, <select>, <textarea>) and validation attributes.
- Implementing form controls and understanding form submission and data handling.
- Using HTML forms in combination with client-side scripting (e.g., JavaScript) for enhanced interactivity.

9. Understanding of Web Semantics and SEO

Outcome: Students use a foundational understanding of web semantics and how HTML contributes to SEO.

Skills Acquired

- Utilizing semantic tags to improve web content readability and search engine optimization.
- Implementing proper heading structures for better content organization and SEO.
- Understanding the role of HTML in improving search engine ranking and visibility.

10. Experience with Project-Based Learning

Outcome: Students have gained practical experience through project-based learning, applying their HTML knowledge to real-world scenarios.

Skills Acquired

- Developing and presenting a complete HTML-based project, such as a personal website or a web application.
- Collaborating with peers or working individually to build functional web pages.
- Applying problem-solving skills to overcome challenges encountered during project development.

To understand structured data, markup languages, systematic analysis art, and manipulation of data, students should be given some intensive games.

Conclusion

Teaching HTML effectively leads to several key outcomes for learners. Students can master basic HTML syntax and structure, including tags, attributes, and elements. They also understand and use core HTML tags, create structured web pages, and write and validate HTML code to conform to web standards. They can also create and format well-structured and styled web pages, organise content into sections, use semantic HTML, insert and format images and links, and implement basic forms for user input.

Works Cited and Recommended Readings

Gerardus Blokdyk. *Markup Language the Ultimate Step-By-Step Guide.* 5starcooks, 2018.

Sowa, John F. *Knowledge Representation.* Cengage Learning, 2000.

Tittel, Ed, et al. *HTML, XHTML & CSS for Dummies.* Wiley, 2011, www.wiley.com/en-us/HTML%2C+XHTML+and+CSS+For+Dummies%2C+7th+Edition-p-9780470916599. Accessed 11 Sept. 2024.

Witt, Andreas, and Dieter Metzing. *Linguistic Modeling of Information and Markup Languages.* Springer Science & Business Media, 2010.

CHAPTER SIX

Teaching Classification and Systems Theories

I recommend to prescribe Sperber G Mcqueen's "Classification and its Structures" for its critical reading in the classroom. The text describes the worldview embodied in a classification system.

Introduction

Classification and systems theories are frameworks used to understand and organize complex information and phenomena in various fields. Classification theory organizes objects, concepts, or phenomena into categories based on shared attributes or criteria, simplifying the analysis and understanding of complex entities. Key concepts include categories and taxonomies, hierarchical structures, and criteria for classification. Applications include biology, library science, and information systems. Systems theory is an interdisciplinary approach that studies complex systems by focusing on their components, interactions, and relationships. Key concepts include inputs, processes, outputs, feedback, types of systems, and system dynamics. Applications include engineering, biology, social sciences, and information systems.

Classification Theory is used in taxonomy, data organization, library systems, and more, while Systems Theory is applied in engineering, biology, social sciences, and information systems. Teaching Classification and

Systems Theories involves defining core concepts, discussing their historical development, using practical applications and examples, engaging students in interactive learning activities, assessing students' understanding and application, and introducing tools for modelling systems and classifying data.

Understanding and teaching classification and systems theories provide valuable insights into organizing knowledge and managing complex interactions, enhancing problem-solving and analytical skills in various disciplines.

Sperberg-McQueen's "Classification and its Structures"

Sperberg-McQueen writes that classification is the assignment of objects to a class in concerned groups. "Classification serves two purposes: by grouping objects" with similar "properties together into a class" and "by separating objects with unlike properties into separate classes, it distinguishes between things that are different in ways relevant to the purpose of the classification. The classification scheme itself can make explicit a particular view concerning the nature of the objects being classified. "Classification in the broad sense involves the correct identification of the properties of the objects of study and is hardly distinguishable from coherent discourse in general. For computer applications in the humanities, classification most often involves either the application of pre-existing classification schemes or the post hoc identification of" clusters among a sample of texts, "parts of texts, bibliography entries, words, or extra-textual events or individuals. Pure classification would require and exhibit perfect knowledge of the object being classified, as it locates each topic in a field in an n-dimensional space near other related topics and distant from unrelated topics. Classification schemes carry a great deal of theoretical interest in addition to their practical utility". (McQueen)

Organising data is essential for computer processing because digital files possess an intrinsic structure due to their encoding. However, the notion of structure can be expanded to encompass higher levels of organisation and is not confined just to the methods by which data streams are divided, recognised, or annotated. Classification systems are highly effective at organising knowledge. Classification systems are utilised in digital settings for many purposes, such as organising the content of a website, arranging data within a system, and assigning names to digital items and their corresponding physical elements. Classification systems introduce a secondary level of organisation into any domain of items, such as texts, physical objects, files, photographs, recordings, and so on. Classification systems are utilised to discern and categorise information, as well as to construct conceptual frameworks. The relationship between these knowledge models and cognitive processes, especially in connection to cultural disparities and bodily encounters, is intricate, yet it is inherent in every instance of naming or organising. All classification systems inherently possess an ideological bias and are not value-neutral, impartial, or self-evident.

Give Exercises

a. Pay attention to the topic taking any excerpt from Jorge Luis Borges explores the categorization of animals based on their various characteristics. The author presents a list of distinct groups, including animals that are owned by the Emperor, animals that have been preserved through embalming, animals that have been trained, young pigs that are still nursing, mythical creatures like mermaids, extraordinary creatures, stray dogs, animals that are specifically mentioned in this classification, animals that exhibit trembling behaviour resembling madness, countless animals, animals that have been depicted with great precision using a delicate camel's-hair brush, other unspecified animals, animals that have recently caused damage to a flower vase, and animals that appear similar to flies when seen from a distance.
b. Michel Foucault(Foucault; Faubion) utilised that excerpt to delve into a philosophical contemplation regarding the foundations upon which knowledge might be established. He inquired about the cognitive processes involved in perceiving equivalence, likeness, and difference/ distinction. The level of specificity and granularity in distinguishing different elements determines the level of sophistication of a categorization system. However, it also incorporates underlying assumptions into its structure. Could you illustrate? Classification systems emerge from various disciplines. Carolus Linnaeus, an

18th-century Swedish botanist, devised a method to categorise plants based on their reproductive organs. Several of the linkages he established and named have been refuted by evidence of the genetic ties among species. However, his system continues to be utilised and remains valuable, as its principles offer a consistent and standardised framework. Classification systems are utilised in many areas of human endeavour and have been the subject of philosophical contemplation across all cultures and periods.

c. Classification systems are essential for naming and organising digital information. Furthermore, we employ intricate systems of nomenclature and categorization that encode information about things and/or areas of knowledge. Organising a collection of music recordings based just on the length of the individual soundtracks would render it impossible to locate works by a specific artist, composer, or conductor. While idiosyncratic or unique schemes of organisation may be effective for an individual, standardised systems of classification are necessary when it comes to sharing information and expertise.
d. Use any tools you know to perform Word Cloud, Pre-process Text and Visualization of the above text/any text of the above philosopher.
e. A space alien archaeologist is examining UCLA students for a museum show on Earth. Each student should put something from their daily routine on the table (one per class). Create a classification system in groups of 4-6 to help the poor alien. You classify them how? Colour, size, order, materials, function, value, OTHER? Always remember that you are promoting UCLA student life in your organisation. Evaluate classification systems and principles.
f. Imagine everyone leaves and the doors explode when closed. The police discover bombs in a table object. Finding the owner of a blue knapsack is the forensic team's goal. Is your classification system useful? How, and why not? How does that explain classification schemes?

Systems Theory

Definition: Systems theory is an interdisciplinary approach that studies complex systems by focusing on their components, interactions, and the relationships between them. It aims to understand how systems function as a whole and how they respond to changes.

Basic Concepts

System Components

Inputs: Resources or information that enter the system.

Processes: Activities or transformations that occur within the system.

Outputs: Results or products produced by the system.

Feedback: Information about the output that is used to adjust and improve the system.

Types of Systems

Open Systems: Systems that interact with their environment and exchange information or resources. Example: An organization that adapts to market changes.

Closed Systems: Systems that are isolated from their environment and do not interact with it. Example: A sealed mechanical device.

System Dynamics

Feedback Loops: Mechanisms where outputs of a system are fed back into the system as inputs to regulate and control its behaviour. For example, a thermostat regulating temperature.

Homeostasis: The ability of a system to maintain stability through self-regulation. Example: The human body's regulation of internal temperature.

Applications

Engineering: Control systems and network design.

Biology: Ecosystems and biological organisms.

Social Sciences: Organizations and social systems.

Information Systems: Computer networks and information processing systems.

Comparing Classification and Systems Theories

Purpose

Classification Theory: Focuses on organizing and categorizing entities based on common attributes to simplify understanding and analysis.

Systems Theory: Focuses on understanding and managing complex interactions and dynamics within systems to optimize performance and adaptability.

Approach

Classification Theory: Emphasizes categorization, hierarchical structures, and criteria-based grouping.

Systems Theory: Emphasizes components, processes, interactions, and feedback mechanisms within systems.

Applications

Classification Theory: Used in taxonomy, data organization, library systems, and more.

Systems Theory: Applied in engineering, biology, social sciences, and information systems.

Teaching Classification and Systems Theories

1. Introduction and Theoretical Background

Define the core concepts and principles.

Discuss the historical development and significance of these theories.

2. Practical Applications and Examples

Use real-world examples and case studies to illustrate how classification and systems theories are applied in various fields.

3. Interactive Learning

Engage students in activities like categorizing objects, creating system models, and analyzing real-world systems.

4. Assessment and Feedback

Use quizzes, assignments, and projects to assess students' understanding and application of these theories.

5. Technology and Tools

Introduce tools for modelling systems and classifying data, such as software for creating system diagrams and classification frameworks.

Understanding and teaching classification and systems theories provide valuable insights into organizing knowledge and managing complex interactions, enhancing problem-solving and analytical skills in various disciplines.

Digital Ontologies, Metadata and Classification

You can prescribe Ramesh Srinivasan and J. Wallack's "Local-Global: Reconciling Mismatched Ontologies" which replies to the questions like:

a. How does a database enact a politics of knowledge?
b. What is the digital and learning divide?
c. What is digital citizenship and democracy?

Ontology is a subdivision of metaphysics that focuses on the fundamental nature of existence. Ontology, in practical terms, refers to a collection of concepts and categories within a specific subject area or domain. It serves to illustrate the features of these concepts and categories, as well as the relationships that exist between them. Ontology is the study of the compatible or incompatible links between the nature or properties of an item or being. "Local-Global: Reconciling Mismatched Ontologies in Development Information Systems"(Schreibman et al.; Holdcroft; Singh) expands upon existing conceptualizations of the digital divide to explore the significant problem of discrepancies between the ontologies of information systems created by the government and the way local communities represent their environments. The trade-off between data comparability across different periods and locations, as well as data compatibility with state administrative requirements, results in a loss of knowledge regarding the context and individuals that policymakers aim to influence. We contend that the harmonisation of community and state ideologies and perspectives is crucial for successful involvement with communities, as well as the creation and execution of development strategies. We propose several approaches to address the issue of mismatched ontologies: implementing educational and communication strategies to facilitate the translation between different ontologies and bridge important gaps; reallocating policy responsibilities to reduce information loss; and establishing mechanisms that allow communities to actively participate in the development of shared ontologies. (Evers; Drucker, "Digital Ontologies: The Ideality of Form in/and Code Storage: Or: Can Graphesis Challenge Mathesis?"; Berry and Fagerjord) Digital ontology, hence, tells about the relations of nature or property of a digital object with others. Metadata is organized and descriptive information that aids in retrieving, utilizing, and managing information resources. It's crucial in distributed network environments like the Internet and within organizations. Examples include cataloguing systems in libraries and software systems. A metadata standard aims to establish a shared understanding of data's significance, ensuring accurate use and interpretation by owners and users. (Drucker, "Digital Ontologies: The Ideality of Form in/and Code Storage: Or: Can Graphesis Challenge Mathesis?")

Classification systems

Metadata is commonly described as information about data. Metadata refers to organised and descriptive information that facilitates the retrieval, utilisation, and management of an information resource. It is particularly relevant in distributed network environments such as the Internet or within organisations. An exemplary illustration of metadata is the cataloguing system prevalent in libraries, which documents crucial information such as the author, title, subject, and physical placement of a resource on the shelf. Another aspect involves the extraction of information from software systems, specifically about software objects such as data flows, control flows, call mappings, architectures, business rules, business terms, and database schemas. A metadata standard is a prescribed set of guidelines that aims to develop a shared comprehension of the significance or semantics of the data, to guarantee accurate and appropriate utilisation and interpretation of the data by its proprietors and users. To establish a shared comprehension, it is necessary to identify several distinct qualities or properties of the data, commonly referred to as metadata. Classification systems are widely adopted in nearly all disciplines, however, the process of their creation and standardisation is often fraught with intense political dynamics. A classification system encapsulates a complete set of beliefs and values, which may result in favouring one group over another or perpetuating established forms of exploitation or cultural dominance. An awareness of these matters is not only crucial but also informative in its regard, as it showcases the influence of classification systems from different cultures or constituencies, as well as our inherent limitations.

Standards for categorization

Standardisation is a crucial aspect of classification systems. If an item is referred to as a potato on one occasion and a tomato on another, it becomes challenging for someone to determine which ingredients to select for a meal. If you organise your music collection by artist's name followed by title, it may be challenging to locate a missing item. Consistency is of utmost importance. When working with extensive systems utilised by numerous institutional repositories to classify and define their objects, such as the Library of Congress subject headings (LCSH) or the Getty's Art and Architectural Thesaurus (AAT), the need for standardisation becomes more crucial. This is particularly evident in the case of the Getty standards. For institutional repositories to effectively share information, it is imperative that the material is organised in a uniform and standardised way, and that it use established vocabularies.

The concept of standardisation is directly linked to the intended application of the information. Objects can be arranged in a nearly limitless variety of ways, as you have observed. Classifying tools based on their purpose is logical, whereas classifying books based on their subject and/or author is also logical. However, if these classifications were interchanged, they would not be effective.

Classification systems are utilised to systematically arrange collections, ascertain the attributes of things within a system, and assign names or designations to those objects in a uniform manner. They share a considerable and meaningful similarity with taxonomies and ontologies.

Taxonomies are systems of nomenclature. They consist of a carefully chosen and regulated set of words used to label goods or objects. Ontologies are conceptual frameworks that represent and organise knowledge. While it is possible that they may or may not categorise objects, their main function is to arrange data and ideas into a well-organized framework. Attempting to rigidly define these terms - categorization, taxonomy, ontology - is unnecessary as they do not have clear-cut and distinct boundaries. They are not always clearly separate, and frequently bear similarities and can be used interchangeably. Taxonomies are comprehensive compilations of terms or names, while categorization systems delineate the properties and relationships of items inside a given system, and ontologies serve as models for knowledge systems. To boost curiosity, I have some additional information to further perplex you.

Fluid Ontologies: Diplomacy

Srinivasan's essay explores the topic of "fluid ontologies". The significance of classification and description systems, as well as the naming standards they employ, becomes evident. The authors highlight the negative consequences (economic, cultural, and personal) that arise from discrepancies between the official and actual methods used to describe catastrophic events. The classification of items and events significantly impacts the resolution of a scenario involving bio-waste, as well as the effectiveness of dealing with it. It is crucial to identify the involvement of dead animals to handle the situation more efficiently. These disparities extend beyond mere variances in terminology and encompass variations in essence. (Drucker, "Digital Ontologies: The Ideality of Form in/and Code Storage: Or: Can Graphesis Challenge Mathesis?")

Wallach and Srinivasan emphasise that ontologies function as entities and mediate the demarcation of borders among different groups. Additionally, they assert that they serve as "cognitive representations of one's environment." The discrepancy between official and experience classification systems leads to inefficiencies and deficiencies due to information loss during negotiations between various stakeholders and resource managers. As said earlier, metadata refers to the information that describes information, objects, content, or documents. The catalogue entry of a book in the library comprises metadata that assists in determining its relevance and locating it on the shelf. Library records often contain standard bibliographic metadata such as the title, author, publisher, place of publishing, date, and a description of the contents, physical aspects, and other attributes of the object. "Necessity of Big Data Analytics in Social Media for Questioning the Existence and Survival of Women and the Marginalized People" justifies why accuracy and impartial data, databases, and metadata are important for equality in society.(Rahaman and Agarwal)

Metadata standards are established for various information domains in libraries, museums, archives, and record-keeping settings. An issue that arises when working with metadata is determining whether one is describing the object itself or its representation. If you own a photograph of a temple in Athens, captured in 1902 using a glass plate and a box camera, and it is being utilised for educational purposes in the field of architecture, does the metadata in the catalogue entry pertain to the characteristics of the photograph, the characteristics of the temple, or both?

Assign Exercises

- Examine the Getty Art and Architecture Thesaurus (AAT) and the Cataloguing Cultural Objects (CCO) for creating a similar project proposal. Visit the following web projects:
- <http://www.getty.edu/research/tools/vocabularies/aat/>
- <http://cco.vrafoundation.org/ http://dublincore.org/>
- Write a blog post on how Wallach and Srinivasan propose fluid ontologies as a partial solution to the tensions between local knowledge and official meta-ontologies. And how his paper highlights the implications of developing classification systems, particularly about politics and ideological systems. Justify.

Attainments of Outcomes

Classification systems organize knowledge, reflecting ideological and epistemological assumptions. Methods can differ even for the same phenomena, such as morphology vs. genetic data. The student understands that metadata refers to the descriptive information that provides details about a set of data. It explains the information included within a document, project, or file. The coexistence of folksonomies and taxonomies can create a productive tension by combining crowd-sourced and user-generated metadata with the standards that evolve within communities of practice.

Works Cited and Recommended Readings

C. M. Sperberg-McQueen, "Classification and its Structures," in Susan Schreibman, Ray Siemens, and John Unsworth eds., *Companion to Digital Humanities* (Oxford: Blackwell Publishing Professional, 2004), <https://companions.digitalhumanities.org/DH/?chapter=content/9781405103213_chapter_14.html>

Drucker, Johanna. "Digital Ontologies: The Ideality of Form in/and Code Storage: Or: Can Graphesis Challenge Mathesis?" *Leonardo*, vol. 34, no. 2, 2001, pp. 141–45. *JSTOR*, http://www.jstor.org/stable/1577017. Accessed 4 Dec. 2023.

Floridi, Luciano. "Against Digital Ontology." *Synthese*, vol. 168, no. 1, 2009, pp. 151–78. *JSTOR*, http://www.jstor.org/stable/40271246. Accessed 4 Dec. 2023.

R. Srinivasan and J. Wallack, "Local-Global: Reconciling Mismatched Ontologies in Development Information Systems," in 2009 42nd Hawaii International Conference on System Sciences. HICSS-42, Big Island, HI, 2009 pp. 1-10. doi: 10.1109/HICSS.2009.810

CHAPTER SEVEN

TEACHING DATA AND DATABASES

I prescribeStephen Ramsay's "Databases" published in *Blackwell Companion to Digital Humanities* and Michael Christie's "Computer Databases and Aboriginal Knowledge" to reply to the following questions: How does Michael Christie devise aboriginal approaches to represent knowledge? How can aboriginal knowledge/traditional knowledge be a system? Can you apply 'aboriginal ontology and epistemology' to the database?; What is the nature of the 'aboriginal database'?

Introduction

Databases have been a fundamental aspect of human intellectual pursuit for centuries, with their origins in text-based categorization and indexing systems since the Middle Ages. The computerized database emerged alongside the initial use of computers in academic and commercial settings, making the challenge of efficiently storing and retrieving information more complex.

Many Aboriginal parents and grandparents, concerned that the younger generation is not growing up with a strong Indigenous knowledge/identity, endorse the use of computer databases to store texts, photos, videos, maps, lists etc to help with their work of teaching. It would be easy to assume that these digital objects contain knowledge, but they are simply information: a series of ones and zeros. The digital object is a re-presentation or an artefact of an earlier act of knowledge performance/production. Its function in the work of education lies in its incorporation into further episodes of knowledge production as any artefact like a book, a map or a photograph is used when people teach. (Christie)

Humanists have been interested in using database technology due to the intellectual potential associated with these seemingly practical matters. This chapter offers an overview of designing and implementing a basic relational database, focusing on storing fundamental details about books currently available for purchase. The purpose is to simplify the intricacies and peculiarities of real-world data, allowing the technical and conceptual aspects of database architecture to become more apparent. The relational model offers the potential for enhanced capacity to store and access information, as well as an elevated level of critical and methodical self-awareness. In digital humanities, the process of creating something is often just as important as the finished output in terms of its experiential significance to the scholarly pursuit. The primary focus of this chapter is on the design and implementation of database systems using the relational model, which is widely used by both computing humanists and professionals in various research and industry fields. (Christie)

Ramsey says that data refers to a collection of facts, statistics, or information that is represented in a structured or unstructured format. It can be in the form of numbers, text, images, or any other type of digital content. We often overlook the phrase since it is so pervasive. The term "big data" is frequently used and it brings to mind the idea of vast quantities of information organised into distinct units that can be analysed and researched in various fields such as espionage, business, healthcare, population studies, disease control, and public opinion, among others. However, every piece of data originates from deliberate choices regarding its creation. The existence of data is nonexistent in the world. It does not constitute atomistic data that can be quantified and organised, such as cells on a swab or cars on a highway. Alternatively, data is generated by establishing specific parameters for its formation. Before delving into databases and their structural support for different activities, it is necessary to first tackle the fundamental theoretical and practical aspects related to the conception and generation of data.

For example, if we observe our surroundings in the room we are currently in, what specific elements can be measured and quantified? Factors such as room temperature, physical attributes of the space, demographic data of the individuals there, and characteristics of the university, among others. Essentially, every entity that can be quantified can be converted into "data" through the process of observation and measurement. Data refers to any information that may be quantified or defined by parameters.(Christie) However, whatever scale do we employ to acquire this information regarding phenomena? Can we employ a temperature gauge capable of functioning on the sun's surface to discern the disparity between the body temperatures of two individuals? What is the temperature difference between the area near the window and the area near the door? Which scale detects notable disparities? The process of transforming raw phenomena into meaningful descriptions is the objective of data generation, so the term "capta" is more appropriate. The term "data" originates from the Greek word "datum," which translates to "given." Capta implies proactive "capture" and the act of generating or building. Capta elucidates the process of generating quantitative information while recognising the subjective nature of parameterized data. To me, data is a culture of past, present and future ages. Data is everything, everything is data. There are two basic kinds of data: numerical and non-numerical data. Numerical is feasible, countable, mathematical and scientifically attainable, whereas non-numerical data like human emotion and sentiment are not easily countable. They are always in abstract forms. For non-numerical data (I call 'nData') sentiment analysis is required. Words are cognitive representations of human sentiments, hence, analysis of emotion is partially possible.

Data Analysis

Man is information. Information is itself an overview of human existence. Data analysis is essential tool for comprehending occurrences and their significance across different cultures and within them. The process entails converting observable occurrences into measurable entities, such as metres or hours, to comprehend the correlation between spatial aspects and dimensions. Metric standards had distinctive historical origins, including the mediaeval monks' methodologies for dividing the day into periods of brightness and darkness. Temperature data is obtained by empirical methods, however, the Centigrade and Celsius scales use distinct units of measurement. The Fahrenheit scale is a unique scale that is based on human perception and understanding. Data sets and databases are generated utilising established metrics, classifications, categorization methods, and spreadsheets. Databases exist in multiple formats, including flat, relational, object-oriented, and others. They can be categorised based on their contents, function, structure, or other distinguishing features. The quality of a database relies only on its content model, encompassing content kinds such as names, addresses, ages, titles, authors, and publishers(Christie).

The process of establishing a data model entails the definition of content kinds and the establishment of a model that represents their relationships. A spreadsheet is a convenient tool for creating a dataset, as it enables the organisation of information using several criteria such as alphabetical, numerical, chronological, or by size. For StarPaws Pet Talent Agency, the process of developing a spreadsheet entails generating data for ten cards containing pertinent information. Arranging information systematically can effectively tackle the difficulties and benefits associated with organising information in an organised manner. Designing conceptual models of data for humanities domains presents unique challenges, necessitating the careful consideration of data value within different settings.

Spreadsheets are uncomplicated data formats, but they are highly effective tools for analysis, modelling, and enhancing productivity. Spreadsheets were employed in analogue settings to handle, display, and scrutinise data. Utilising a spreadsheet is an effective approach for examining a budget, and implementing automation in this process can be quite advantageous when attempting to forecast the impact of alterations in pay rates or interest rates on expenses. VISICALC, a computerised spreadsheet developed in the late 1970s, gained popularity as the first groundbreaking application that revolutionised the industry. The digital spreadsheet revolutionised the integration of computing into commercial operations. The following are database development milestones:

a. In 1969-70, the LANPAR method was developed. LANPAR stands for "automatic natural order recalculation algorithm". Rene Pardo and Remy Landau
b. 1970-72 Edgar Clogg is studying database ideas. The time period from 1974 to 1976. IBM developed the Query Language (QUEL) in the 1970s for their Relational Database Management System (RDBMS).
c. Around 1979 VISICALC, developed by Dan Bricklin and Bob Frankston, is sometimes referred to as a "killer app". Apple and IBM
d. Lotus 1-2-3 from the 1980s
e. The SQL (Structured Query Language) used in the 1980s is commonly referred to as Sequel.

Exercise StarPaws

A spreadsheet has numerous advantages compared to a card catalogue or Rolodex, therefore it is classified as a "flat" database. The entirety of the information is contained within a single table. A relational database partitions data into many tables interconnected by keys. These allow for the categorization of data based on relationships. A key characteristic of relational databases is their ability to accommodate dependent variations in data (such as when a dog's owner changes, resulting in a change in the associated telephone number) as well as independent variations (such as when multiple dogs perform the same role in a film, where the role remains constant but the relationship to the animal may differ). When organising your cards and/or spreadsheets, you need to determine which pieces of information should be grouped together in tables and which ones should be kept separate. What is the reason? You have the ability to create a visual representation of this concept using a sheet of paper and a writing instrument.

The concepts for building a database in software programmes such as Access, Filemaker, MySQL, or any other, are fundamentally the same for all relational databases. However, alternative database designs exist that rely not only on an entity-relationship model but also on other principles. Examine object-oriented databases, RDF formats, and linked open data (LOD). When constructing a database, you are responsible for formulating the content model, establishing fields for data input, and designing the interconnections. Next, you construct a form-based interface to input data into the database. The organisation of this database may be significantly altered to enhance its utility and coherence. Acquiring the skills to alter data via searches/queries, reports, and other techniques will demonstrate the significance of a database in effectively managing information and metadata.

The fundamental tenets of database administration and design encompass modularity, data modelling for content type definition, establishing relations, and the subsequent utilisation of data through selection and display. Given that all data is captured as a construct through interpretation, databases serve as influential rhetorical tools that frequently present themselves as unbiased observations or records of events, information, or objects in the environment.

Assign Exercises

1. Michael Christie's article explores the limitations of database structures in expressing cultural materials, arguing for narrative and multi-dimensional forms. He proposes a concept of 'Indigenous database':
2. An Indigenous database must be a lot more than simply a conventional database full of representations of Aboriginal knowledge. For it to be an Indigenous database, its architecture and structure, its search processes and interfaces, its ownership and uses must also reflect and support context-specific indigenous ways of being and knowing, and people's control over their knowledge. (Christie)
3. He discusses the connection between these issues and the Wallack and Srinivasan essay, highlighting the need for non-linear, multi-dimensional forms. Taking this into consideration present your ideas on the following:

- "Digital songlines"
- "Kinship embedded in the system"
- "Cartesian philosophy oval/mathematics"
- "Storyworld" not "storyline"

4. Work on the history of the database to find similar projects on the subject.

Computing History Organization's History of Database (a site with good conceptual information) available at <http://www.comphist.org/computing_history/new_page_9.htm>.

Nature of 'Aboriginal database' and its value

M. Christie asserts that the optimal databases for Indigenous communities to utilise for their specific knowledge needs. "The best databases for indigenous peoples to use for their purposes of knowledge transmission may be frustratingly difficult or counter-intuitive for western scientists to use." Western scientists may find the use of transmission to be challenging or unintuitive. It is conceivable to develop a system that caters to the objectives and perspectives of both indigenous communities and non-indigenous interest groups. However, to adequately respect the rights and responsibilities of Indigenous intellectual property owners and custodians, as well as their objectives, The intergenerational transmission of Indigenous knowledge and Indigenous ownership are key factors. The ease of use should not be sacrificed to accommodate the imagined requirements of non-indigenous partners for simple and instinctive access. By employing "aboriginal ontology and epistemology," it is possible to create easily accessible databases that are primarily intended for indigenous groups to manage and utilise their digital material. In the future, Indigenous adults may utilise digital technology to impart valuable knowledge to Indigenous youth(Christie).

Attainment of Outcomes

Databases facilitate the implementation of authority control, ensuring uniformity and standardisation across extensive collections of information. There are two types of databases: flat and relational databases. Flat databases establish a framework that enables the storage of content based on its category. Relational databases enable the management and manipulation of information based on its dependent or independent relationship. Out of these two, learners can set up examples of the 'aboriginal dataset' as discussed by Christie.

Works Cited and Recommended Readings

Christie, Michae "Computer Databases and Aboriginal Knowledge" available at <https://www.cdu.edu.au/centres/ik/pdf/CompDatAbKnow.pdf>Accessed on 4 December 2023.

David Kroenke, David Auer, *Database Processing: Fundamentals, Design, and Implementation*, 12th Edition. Publisher: Prentice Hall, 2011

Hunter, L. *Fact - Information - Data - Knowledge: Databases as a Way of Organizing Knowledge. Literary and Linguistic Computing* 5: 49–57. 1990.

Kroenke, David M, et al *Database Concepts*. Pearson. 2017.

Rahaman, V. *A Textbook on Databases in Digital Humanities*. Chennai:Notion Press, 2024. <https://www.barnesandnoble.com/w/a-textbook-on-databases-in-digital-humanities-valiur-rahaman/1146285638?ean=9798895449202>

Stephen Ramsay. Databases. A Companion to Digital Humanities. Blackwell. Available at <https://companions.digitalhumanities.org/DH/?chapter=content/9781405103213_chapter_15.html>

CHAPTER EIGHT

Teaching Data Narrative and Storytelling Framework

I prescribe reading marvellous essays Lev Manovich's "Database as Symbolic Form" and Ed Folsom's “Database as Genre” They clarify how a Data Storytelling Framework career involves transforming data into compelling narratives to inform and drive decision-making.

Introduction

This field combines data analysis, visualization, and storytelling skills and can be applied across various industries. Key responsibilities include analyzing data, designing visualizations, crafting narratives, and communicating findings to stakeholders. Required educational background includes data science, statistics, computer science, communications, and design. Developing skills include data analysis, visualization, storytelling, communication, and technical skills. Career opportunities include finance, healthcare, marketing, and technology. Future trends include increased demand for data-driven decision-making and interdisciplinary roles.

Data Storytelling Framework

It should be clear to teachers that a Data Storytelling Framework is a structured method for transforming data into compelling narratives that communicate insights, drive decision-making, and engage audiences. It involves defining the objective, analyzing the data, crafting the narrative, designing visualizations, integrating storytelling techniques, reviewing and refining the narrative, and presenting and communicating the data story. This approach can effectively drive understanding, action, and engagement in data-driven decision-making. Hence, they must introduce the basics of DSF. Let us understand how a Data Storytelling Framework is an applied method for transforming data into compelling narratives, combining analysis, visualization, and storytelling principles (Chein and Marie-Laure Mugnier). Instruct students stepwise:

1. Define Your Objective

- Purpose: Clearly articulate the goal of your data story. What do you want to achieve or convey?
- Identify the Problem or Question: What specific issue or question is the data addressing?
- Target Audience: Who is the intended audience? Understand their needs, interests, and level of expertise.

2. Analyze the Data

- Exploration: Thoroughly explore the data to understand its structure, quality, and key insights.
- Data Collection: Gather relevant and high-quality data.
- Data Cleaning: Prepare the data by cleaning and organizing it to ensure accuracy.
- Exploratory Data Analysis (EDA): Use statistical and visual techniques to identify patterns, trends, and anomalies.

3. Craft the Narrative

- Structure: Develop a clear and engaging narrative structure that guides the audience through the data story.
- Introduction (Context): Set the stage by providing background information and context. Explain why the data is relevant and important.
- Body (Findings): Present the key insights and findings from the data. Organize this section logically, using visualizations and explanations to support your points.
- Conclusion (Implications): Summarize the main takeaways and their implications. Provide recommendations or actions based on the data.

4. Design Visualizations

- Visualization: Create visual representations that enhance understanding and engagement.
- Choose the Right Visuals: Select appropriate types of charts, graphs, maps, or infographics based on the data and message. Common types include bar charts, line graphs, pie charts, and scatter plots (Chein and Marie-Laure Mugnier).
- Best Practices: Follow best practices for data visualization, such as clarity, simplicity, and avoiding misleading representations.
- Interactive Elements: Consider adding interactive elements (e.g., dashboards) to allow users to explore the data further.

5. Integrate Storytelling Techniques

- Engagement: Use storytelling techniques to make the data relatable and memorable.
- Narrative Arc: Craft a narrative arc with a beginning, middle, and end. Start with an engaging hook, develop the story with key insights, and conclude with a compelling ending.
- Human Element: Incorporate personal stories, anecdotes, or case studies to make the data more relatable and impactful.
- Visual and Emotional Appeal: Use visual and emotional elements to enhance the storytelling experience and connect with the audience.

6. Review and Refine

- Feedback: Review the data story for accuracy, coherence, and effectiveness.
- Peer Review: Seek feedback from colleagues or stakeholders to ensure the narrative is clear and impactful.
- Refinement: Make necessary adjustments based on feedback to improve the clarity and effectiveness of the data story.

7. Present and Communicate

- Delivery: Choose the most effective medium and method for presenting the data story.
- Formats: Present the data story through reports, presentations, dashboards, or interactive websites.
- Communication Style: Tailor your communication style to the audience, ensuring that the story is accessible and engaging.

8. Framework in Action

- Objective: Illustrate the impact of a new marketing strategy on sales performance.
- Define Objective: Demonstrate how the marketing strategy increased sales and identify which channels were most effective.
- Analyze Data: Collect sales data before and after the strategy implementation. Clean the data, perform trend analysis, and identify key metrics.

9. Craft the Narrative

- Introduction: Explain the marketing strategy and its goals.
- Body: Present data on sales performance, using charts to show changes over time and comparisons between different channels.
- Conclusion: Summarize the success of the strategy and provide recommendations for future marketing efforts.

10. Design Visualizations

- Use line graphs to show sales trends over time.
- Create bar charts to compare sales performance across different marketing channels.
- Incorporate interactive dashboards to allow stakeholders to explore the data further.
- Integrate Storytelling Techniques:
- Include a case study or testimonial from a customer affected by the marketing strategy.
- Use a narrative arc to guide the audience through the data story.

11. Review and Refine

- Get feedback from team members and revise the narrative and visuals as needed.
- Present and Communicate:
- Prepare a presentation with slides and interactive elements to share with stakeholders.

In this way, one can instruct students to transform data into a compelling story that drives understanding, action, and engagement.

Examples of Data Storytelling Frameworks

It illustrates how data can be used to craft compelling narratives. Here are a few notable frameworks, each tailored to different types of data storytelling needs:

1. The Data-Driven Storytelling Framework

Purpose: To create a structured approach to crafting a narrative from data, ensuring that key insights are communicated effectively. Instruct to follow the steps:

Context and Objective

- Define the purpose of the data story and the audience's needs.
- Example: Analyzing the impact of a new product launch on customer satisfaction.

Data Collection and Preparation

- Gather relevant data and clean it for analysis.
- Example: Collect customer feedback surveys before and after the product launch.

Exploration and Analysis

- Analyze the data to identify key trends and insights.
- Example: Use statistical methods to find changes in satisfaction levels.

Narrative Development

- Introduction: Provide context about the product launch and its goals.
- Body: Present key findings using visualizations (e.g., bar charts showing changes in satisfaction scores).
- Conclusion: Summarize the impact and suggest recommendations for future product improvements.

- Visualization and Presentation: Create visualizations to support the narrative and present them in an engaging format.
- Example: Interactive dashboards showing satisfaction scores across different demographics.
- Review and Feedback: Refine the story based on feedback from stakeholders.

2. The Storytelling with Data Framework

Purpose: To emphasize the importance of combining data analysis with effective storytelling techniques. Instruct to follow the steps:

Understand the Audience

- Tailor the narrative to the audience's interests and expertise level.
- Example: Presenting sales data to senior executives versus a technical team.

Craft the Narrative Arc

- Beginning: Set the stage with background information and context.
- Example: Describe the market conditions leading up to the sales period.
- Middle: Present the main findings with supporting data.
- Example: Use line charts to show sales trends over time.
- End: Conclude with actionable insights and recommendations.
- Example: Suggest strategies to capitalize on successful sales trends.

Design Effective Visualizations

- Choose the right type of visualization to support the narrative.
- Example: Heat maps to show sales performance by region.

Engage and Persuade

- Use storytelling techniques such as anecdotes, analogies, and visuals to make the data relatable and memorable.
- Example: Share a success story from a satisfied customer to illustrate positive sales outcomes.
- Iterate and Improve: Collect feedback and refine the narrative for clarity and impact.

3. The Data Storytelling Canvas

- Purpose: To provide a visual tool for organizing and structuring data stories.

Components

Objective: Define the main goal of the data story.

- Example: Assessing the effectiveness of a marketing campaign.

Audience: Identify who will be consuming the data story and their needs.

- Example: Marketing team needing insights on campaign performance.

Key Messages: Determine the core messages you want to convey.

- Example: Increased engagement and improved ROI from the campaign.

Data Sources: List the data sources used for analysis.

- Example: Social media analytics, sales data, and customer feedback.

Insights and Findings: Summarize key insights derived from the data.

- Example: A significant increase in website traffic and conversions.

Visualization Plan: Outline the types of visualizations to use.

- Example: Pie charts for engagement metrics and bar graphs for conversion rates.

Narrative Structure: Define the structure of the story (Introduction, Body, Conclusion).

- Example: Introduce the campaign, present performance data, and conclude with recommendations.

Feedback and Revision: Incorporate feedback and revise the narrative as needed.

4. The TED Talk Model

The aims is to craft a persuasive data story inspired by TED Talk techniques.

Instruct to Follow the Steps

- Hook: Start with a compelling opening to capture attention.

Example: Present a surprising statistic or anecdote related to the data.

- Problem Statement: Clearly define the problem or question addressed by the data.

Example: Highlight a significant issue or challenge faced by the organization.

- Data Exploration: Share insights and findings using visualizations.

Example: Use infographics and charts to illustrate key data points.

- Solution and Impact: Present the proposed solution or recommendations based on the data.

Example: Suggest actionable steps to address the problem and show potential outcomes.

- Call to Action: End with a powerful call to action or a thought-provoking question.

Example: Encourage the audience to implement changes or consider new strategies.

Each of these frameworks provides a structured approach to data storytelling, ensuring that the data is presented in a clear, engaging, and actionable way. By following these frameworks, you can create narratives that effectively communicate data insights and drive decision-making.

The database and narrative are fundamentally contrasting as the former is essentially disordered while the latter is organically structured. Michael Christie has rightly observed, "Databases are not innocent objects. They carry within them particular culturally and historically contingent assumptions about the nature of the world, and the nature of knowledge; what it is, and how it can be preserved and renewed."(Christie)

Data structures and algorithms are fundamental components that shape various aspects of computer culture. CD-ROMs, websites, and other forms of new media that are structured like databases align with the data structure, whereas narratives, such as computer games, align with the algorithms. In simple terms, a database may be likened to a data structure, just as a narrative can be likened to an algorithm. Generally, the act of producing a work in new media can be perceived as the development of an interface to a database. Traditionally, the artist created a distinctive piece of art using a certain media. Thus, there was no distinction between the interface and the job; in essence, the interface lacked a discernible level. Through the utilisation of new media, the content of the work and the interface are rendered distinct from each other. Hence, it is feasible to generate diverse interfaces for the identical substance. The novel media entity comprises one or more interfaces to a database of multimedia content.(Kitchin; Kim; Gutierrez; Christie; Cheney-Lippold) To elucidate the differentiation between database and story, it is crucial to explicitly define the term "narrative." To be considered a narrative, an object must meet the following criteria:

a. The composition must include both an actor and a narration.
b. The text must encompass the various layers of text, tale, and fabula [creator].
c. It must consist of "a sequence of interconnected occurrences brought about or encountered by individuals."

Databases serve as the foundation for narratives, providing a user interface for accessing information. They can be either linear or hyper-narrative, with a hyper-narrative having multiple choices for the reader. Lev Manovich's work "Database as Symbolic Form" highlights the importance of examining syntagmatic and paradigmatic dimensions when analyzing the role of databases and narratives. Databases can store metadata and can serve as the main document, while narratives are linear. The PMLA, a publication by the Modern Language Association, sparked debate on the relationship between databases and narratives. Some argue that databases are non-linear, while narratives are linear, and that combinatorial labor and content models are essential components of human communication. The debate revolves around the definition of discourse, human speech, and the regulations and norms governing its ability to document both real and imaginary experiences. (D'Ignazio and Klein; Eubanks; Dontha; Berlowitz; Rahaman and Haider; Rahaman and Bhat; Marr)

Assignments

1. Ask students to use/misuse of data.

2. Teach/Read the following essays in connection with Lev Manovich, "Database as Symbolic Form" (1999)

- Ed Folsom, "Database as Genre: The Epic Transformation of the Archives" (2007)
- Jerome McGann, "Database, Interface, and Archival Fever" (2007)

3. Develop a flowchart of textual interpretation on:

- Conflicts regarding one's identity, description, or existence

- Differentiations between the tangible structure and the digital representation
- Continuities and ruptures: absence of novelty against complete novelty
- Technodystopia, teleology, and liberatory utopianism are concepts that pertain to the influence of technology on society, the study of purpose or end goals, and the belief in a future society that is free and ideal.

4. Can you map the elements in Omeka and your projects to the basic features of digital humanities projects? What is still missing and/or unexplained in the creation of these projects?

Conclusion

Traditionally, artists created unique pieces of art using specific media, but new media allows for diverse interfaces. Databases serve as the foundation for narratives, providing a user interface. The relationship between databases and narratives is debated, with some arguing they are non-linear and others arguing they are linear.

Works Cited and Recommended Readings

Beshero-Bondar, Elisa, and Kellie Donovan-Condron. "Modelling Mary Russell Mitford's Networks: The Digital Mitford as Collaborative Database." *Women's Literary Networks and Romanticism: "A Tribe of Authoresses,"* edited by Andrew O. Winckles and Angela

Chein, Michel, and Marie-Laure Mugnier. *Graph-Based Knowledge Representation.* Springer Science & Business Media, 2008.

Folsom, Ed. "Database as Genre: The Epic Transformation of Archives." *PMLA*, vol. 122, no. 5, 2007, pp. 1571–79. *JSTOR*, http://www.jstor.org/stable/25501803. Accessed 4 Dec. 2023.

Freedman, Jonathan. "Whitman, Database, Information Culture." *PMLA*, vol. 122, no. 5, 2007, pp. 1596–602. *JSTOR*, http://www.jstor.org/stable/25501807. Accessed 4 Dec. 2023.

Hayles, N. Katherine. "Narrative and Database: Natural Symbionts." *PMLA*, vol. 122, no. 5, 2007, pp. 1603–08. *JSTOR*, http://www.jstor.org/stable/25501808. Accessed 4 Dec. 2023.

McGann, Jerome. "Database, Interface, and Archival Fever." *PMLA*, vol. 122, no. 5, 2007, pp. 1588–92. *JSTOR*, http://www.jstor.org/stable/

25501805. Accessed 4 Dec. 2023.

Manovich, Lev. “Database as Symbolic Form.” In Database Aesthetics: Art in the Age of Information Overflow, edited by Victoria Vesna, 39-60. Minneapolis: University of Minnesota Press, 2007.

Rahaman, V., Haider, A. "Deconstructive Big Data Analytics: Literary Texts Analysis Through Atlas.ti Software". In: Sharma, S., Rahaman, V., Sinha, G.R. (eds) *Big Data Analytics in Cognitive Social Media and Literary Texts.* Springer, 2021. Singapore. https://doi.org/10.1007/978-981-16-4729-1_3

Rahaman, V. *A Textbook on Databases in Digital Humanities.* Chennai:Notion Press, 2024. Available at <https://www.amazon.in/Textbook-Databases-Digital-Humanities-Non-Engineering/>

Rehbein, Liverpool University Press, 2017, pp. 137–95. *JSTOR*, https://doi.org/10.2307/j.ctt1ps32xn.10. Accessed 4 Dec. 2023.

CHAPTER NINE

Teaching Information Visualization (InfoViz)

I prescribe Rose Plaisant's "Exploring Erotics in Emily Dickinson's Correspondence with Text Mining and Visual Interfaces" for understanding Information visualization is a crucial field that uses graphical techniques to transform complex data into understandable insights, facilitating better communication and decision-making across various domains; and to share answers to define the appropriateness of InfoVis with essentials of InfoVis?

Introduction

Teaching Information Visualization (InfoViz) aims to equip students with the skills and knowledge to create, interpret, and utilize visual representations of data. The objectives include understanding the principles of information visualization, developing technical skills, applying visualization techniques, evaluating visualization effectiveness, understanding data representation, promoting effective communication, addressing ethical and design considerations, and encouraging innovation and creativity. The objectives include understanding the fundamental principles of information visualization, acquiring technical skills, applying visualization techniques, evaluating visualization effectiveness, understanding data representation, promoting effective communication, addressing ethical and design considerations, and encouraging innovation and creativity. By focusing on these areas, educators can prepare students to excel in creating effective, insightful, and responsible data visualizations, enhancing their ability to communicate complex information clearly and compellingly. The curriculum also includes hands-on projects, case studies, and peer review processes to help students apply visualization techniques to real-world data and problems. By addressing ethical issues and promoting inclusive design, students can enhance their ability to handle different types of data and visualization challenges.

InfoVis

InfoVis is an emerging field of study that centres on employing visualisation methods to aid individuals in comprehending and examining data. In this lesson, we will work through various presentations of data and compare them to see if the rhetorical force of each visual format becomes clear, as well as examples of where a particular chart, graph, or diagram simply does not work. The effective use of different graphical forms is an art, and though it has no easy rules, it is governed by basic principles (as per the previous session). Information visualization is a process that involves creating visual representations of data and information to aid in understanding, analyzing, and making informed decisions. It enables users to explore and interact with data, identify patterns, trends, and anomalies, and communicate findings effectively. Key aspects of information visualization include data exploration, communication, and decision-making.

Various types of visualizations include charts, graphs, maps, dashboards, infographics, networks and trees. Effective visualizations should be clear, accurate, simple, relevant, and interactive. Tools and software for creating effective visualizations include Tableau, Microsoft Power BI, D3.js, Excel, and Google Data Studio. Applications of information visualization include business intelligence, healthcare, finance, public policy, and education. The process of creating effective visualizations involves defining objectives, preparing data, choosing a visualization type, designing and building the visualization, and testing and refining it. Examples of effective visualizations include sales dashboards, COVID-19 data maps, customer journey maps, and financial performance reports.

Teaching Information Visualization aims to equip students with the skills and knowledge to effectively present and interpret data visually. Key learning outcomes include understanding visualization principles, proficiency with visualization tools and software, ability to create effective visualizations, data analysis and interpretation, critical evaluation of visualizations, understanding audience and context, communication skills, ethical and legal considerations, interdisciplinary application, and project and teamwork skills. Conceptual knowledge includes understanding the role of visual representation in data analysis and communication, such as data-ink ratio, minimizing chartjunk, data density, and graphical integrity. Students will gain hands-on experience with popular visualization tools and software, such as *Tableau, Power BI, D3.js,* and *Excel*, and be taught to apply these tools to create charts, graphs, dashboards, and interactive visualizations. Visualization types include bar charts, line graphs, scatter plots, heat maps, and more. Students will learn to clean, organize, and prepare data for visualization, extract meaningful insights, and critically evaluate visualizations for accuracy, clarity, and effectiveness. Communication skills include effective presentation and storytelling, ethical considerations, and legal issues related to data privacy and intellectual property. Interdisciplinary application explores how information visualization techniques can be applied across various fields, while project and teamwork skills involve working on group projects and real-world projects.

Hands-on and Class Activity

Utilise a basic dataset consisting of the ages of individuals within your acquaintance, organised in a straightforward spreadsheet format, and present it through a minimum of five distinct visualisations using Many Eyes. Alternatively, employ one of their data sets and replicate the same procedure. Which option is logical? Which ones do not? For what reason? What insights does the exercise provide regarding the rhetoric of information graphics?

Ask to Present Critical Assignments

- Charles Minard's Chart: https://en.wikipedia.org/wiki/File:Minard.png

- Exercise: List the correlated elements in the chart.
- Read the figure "Pioneer Plaque: 1972"
- https://en.wikipedia.org/w/index.php?title=File:Pioneer_plaque.svg&page=1
- Exercise: What is the information being communicated? Suggest changes.
- Best and Worst: http://flowingdata.com/
- Exercise: Name your own best/worst: when do the graphics overwhelm content?

Project related

What is the purpose of data visualisation? The explanations can be categorised into two primary groups: analysis and presentation.

Analytical visualisation is the process of exploring and examining data. During the 1970s, the statistician John Tukey introduced the concept of exploratory data analysis, which involves utilising charts to gain insights into a dataset. To ascertain the information included inside the data, you promptly examine it from multiple perspectives. You own the dual role of both creating and consuming the charts.

Presentative visualisation involves the act of conveying information. You possess a comprehensive understanding of the information conveyed by the data, and you employ visual representations, such as charts, to facilitate comprehension of a dataset by others. You are the creator and your audience is the recipient of the charts.

This session focuses on the concept of presentative visualisation and guides how to effectively alter your approach. The topic concerns the process of visually representing data to effectively convey information to individuals. The focus is on effectively and aesthetically conveying data through communication. You will acquire the knowledge and skills to:

1. Create a design that is tailored to the specific target demographic.
2. Select the appropriate visualisation
3. Create visually comprehensible visuals
4. Consolidate everything

I do not focus on the utilisation of a particular tool but allow students to instruct any software of their choice and concentrate on the design aspect.

- Jacques Bertin: Seven Graphic Principles
- <https://infovis-wiki.net/wiki/Visual_Variables>

Edward Tufte's Display Theory

Edward Tufte's *Visual Display of Quantitative Information* explores the theory and use of data graphics, emphasising that the most efficient method of conveying information about a group of numbers is through visual representations such as statistical graphics, charts, and tables. The book contains 250 pictures showcasing exemplary statistical graphics, along with a limited number of subpar examples. It offers an in-depth analysis of the most effective methods for presenting data, ensuring accuracy, efficiency, and expedited analysis. Additionally, this resource provides details regarding the layout of the high-resolution screens, the utilisation of small multiple images, techniques for altering and enhancing visuals, and the optimisation of the data-ink ratio. The text discusses several types of graphics, including time series, relational graphics, data maps, and multivariate designs. It also explores the detection of graphical deception, including the distinction between design variation and data variation, as well as the origins of deception. Details regarding the field of aesthetics and the presentation of data through graphical displays. Visual Exercise. Superior visual representation, Visual coherence, Origins of visual integrity and refinement, Data Graphics Theory Optimisation of data visualisation and graphic refinement, Chartjunk refers to unnecessary and distracting elements in a chart, such as excessive vibrations, grids, and decorative elements like ducks. Maximising the use of data-ink and optimising graphical design, Polymorphic graphics components, Information density and the use of several tiny visual representations. The study of aesthetics and technical aspects in the design of data graphics, as well as the creation of designs specifically for presenting information. His other book *Envisioning Information* presents a wide array of examples that illustrate the concept of visual thinking, accompanied by exquisitely produced pages. An exquisite delight for individuals who engage in logical thinking and acquire knowledge through visual representations.

His *The Visual Display of Quantitative Information* is a crucial text in the field of data visualization, focusing on the principles of clarity, precision, and integrity. The book emphasizes the importance of minimizing non-essential ink, chartjunk, data density, small multiples, chart design, and graphical integrity. The data-ink ratio is the proportion of a graphic's ink devoted to a non-redundant display of data information. Chartjunk refers to any non-data ink in a chart that does not help the viewer understand the data and might even obscure it. High data density allows viewers to see more information in a compact space, enhancing the depth of insight that can be drawn from the visualization. Small multiples are series of similar graphs or charts that share the same scale and axes, used to compare different subsets of data or different periods in a consistent and easily comparable format. Graphical integrity involves presenting data in a manner that is truthful and accurate, avoiding distortion and ensuring that the visualization faithfully reflects the data's underlying values. Historical context helps viewers understand trends and changes over time, and the effectiveness of visualization depends on how well it communicates to its intended audience. Data presentation techniques include graphical excellence, which involves presenting complex data in a clear, concise, and visually appealing manner, and comparisons, which facilitate comparisons and highlight differences or trends.

Activity

Look at Edward Tufte's first chapter in the *Visual Display of Quantitative Information*, and ask whether or not "form follows data."

Attainments of Outcomes

Understanding the value of feasibility, transparency, accessibility and visual graphics helps society user-friendly techno-citizens. Teaching Information Visualization equips students with skills for data presentation, analysis, critical evaluation, audience awareness, communication, ethical considerations, interdisciplinary application, and project teamwork.

Works Cited and Recommended Readings

Fekete , Jean-Daniel et al (Ed.) *Information Visualization: Human-Centered Issues and Perspectives*. Springer.

Moretti, Franco. *Distant Reading* [1 ed.].Verso. 2013.

Tufte, Edward. *Visual Display of Quantitative Information*. Graphics Press, Year: 2001

CHAPTER TEN

Teaching Data Mining and Text Analysis

Teaching Data Mining and Text Analysis aims to equip students with the skills to extract meaningful insights from large datasets and unstructured text. This area combines statistical analysis, machine learning, and natural language processing techniques.

Key learning outcomes include understanding data mining concepts, data preparation, proficiency with data mining tools and software, programming skills, text analysis methods, advanced data mining techniques, and practical applications. Ethical considerations are also addressed, including data privacy and bias. The learning outcomes include technical skills, analytical skills, application knowledge, ethical awareness, and communication skills. This prepares students to tackle complex data challenges and effectively communicate insights. I prescribe William Turkel's "Data Mining with Criminal Intent" which is available at <http://criminalintent.org/>, <http://criminalintent.org/getting-started/> to instruct solutions to the followingquestions:

1. What is the meaning and role of data mining in humanities?
2. How does the interface to the Old Bailey change from the first to second versions? Demonstrate major concerns.

Introduction

Data mining is a method of analysing a dataset to extract valuable information from it. The provided definition is very broad, encompassing even the basic act of conducting a string search, such as typing into a search box in a library catalogue or a Google window. Extracting quantitative data or statistical information is a common method used in the social sciences. Software tools designed for this purpose have a lengthy track record and come in a range of levels of advancement and intricacy. To obtain a concise and informative introduction to SPSS, a widely used statistical software, I recommend reading the following resource:<http://www.dummies.com/how-to/content/how-spss-statistical-package-for-the-social- scienc.html>

However, data mining in the field of digital humanities typically entails extracting information from a collection of texts and/or their metadata to pose research inquiries that may or may not require quantitative analysis. If you wish to analyse the occurrence rate of the words "she" and "he" in newspaper reports of political speeches during the early 20th century, both before and after the ratification of the 19th Amendment in August 1920, which granted women the right to vote. If you desired to associate these terms with the phrases they were used in organise the outcomes according to other criteria such as frequency, emotional value, attribution, and others. This type of text analysis is a subcategory of data mining. Several technologies have been created for analysing unstructured texts, which refer to texts in standard formats. Text analysis programmes employ techniques such as word counts, keyword density, frequency analysis, and other methodologies to extract significant information. The issue of defining relevant information is a subject of ongoing debate, and text analysis technologies can provide equally absurd outcomes as any other method.

Data Mining ProcessData mining is a systematic process that involves identifying patterns, correlations, and insights from large datasets using various techniques and algorithms. The process begins with problem definition, which aims to define the problem or goal, determine the scope, and establish success criteria. Data collection involves gathering relevant data from various sources, such as databases, spreadsheets, or external sources. Data cleaning ensures data availability and a comprehensive dataset.

Data exploration involves understanding the data's structure, patterns, and initial insights through descriptive statistics, data visualization, and correlation analysis. Feature selection/engineering involves selecting or creating relevant features for data mining models, which can enhance model performance and reduce complexity.

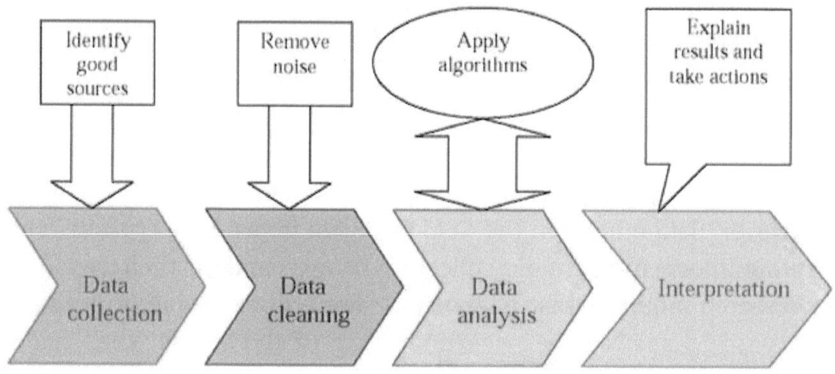

Figure 1: Data Mining Process

Modelling involves applying data mining algorithms to build models that extract patterns and insights from the data. This includes choosing appropriate algorithms, training models, and validating models. Evaluation evaluates the performance of the models, ensuring they meet defined objectives. Deployment involves integrating models into production systems or decision-making processes, monitoring performance, and updating models regularly. Interpretation and reporting involve communicating results and insights to stakeholders. This includes creating detailed reports, visualizing insights, and providing actionable recommendations. Feedback and iteration involve collecting feedback, refining models, and iterating the process to improve results and address any issues.

Make students practise the flowchart Figure 1. following how the data mining process is iterative and involves multiple stages to ensure effective, reliable, and aligned data mining efforts with overall objectives. By carefully managing each stage, organizations and researchers can derive valuable insights and make data-driven decisions.

VisualText

VisualText is an optimal tool for rapidly creating precise and efficient systems for extracting information, processing natural language, and analysing text for even the most intricate requirements. The VisualText IDE can be utilised to automate the process of populating databases with essential content that is now concealed within textual documents. As an illustration, you can extract business happenings from web news sites and generate a searchable database for up-to-date business information. VisualText has been utilised to construct several applications, such as precise analyzers for extracting information from resumes, systems that classify online pages, a monitor for financial transaction chat, email analyzers, selective web crawlers, and additional functionalities. VisualText stands out by allowing non-programmers and non-linguists to develop and improve analyzers. By selecting and emphasising new phrases inside a document, the user can automatically create an improved analyzer. VisualText autonomously produces novel rules and seamlessly integrates them into the analyzer architecture. Our analyzers are transparent, allowing you to build and oversee knowledge, grammar, and algorithms. It is possible to construct a text analyzer completely within VisualText, starting from the beginning and going all the way to the end. Through the process of iteratively altering and testing the analyzer, you may efficiently construct text analyzers without the need to wait for code and rules to compile.

Exercise A

Even a basic tool like Textanalyser, which can be accessed at http://textalyser.net/ can generate valuable results—but for what specific objective? Employ the tool and then identify a context or problem in which it would be beneficial. Examine the various categorizations of analysis. Stop words are frequently used terms in a language that are typically disregarded in text analysis due to their lack of substantial meaning or contribution to the overall comprehension of the text. Which additional features can you manipulate and what influence can they exert on the results? Now analyse a more complex instrument and compare the terminology used to describe its characteristics with that used by Textanalyser. You can access the website at http://www.textanalysis.com/Products/VisualText/visualtext.html

A "conceptual grammar" is a set of rules and principles that control how concepts are organised and represented in language. The developers of this grammar delineate diverse applications in their promotional materials. Text analysis is a method of qualitative research that combines quantitative techniques and search/match algorithms to identify the components and characteristics found in a given text. Is there a genuine paradox between the quantitative and qualitative approaches in text analysis? In 2009, the National Endowment for the Humanities initiated a "digging into data challenge" as part of its efforts to promote digital scholarship. The goal was to develop efficient strategies for engaging with digital projects that involve large amounts of data. Examine the project and review the funded proposals. The link is: <http://www.diggingintodata.org/Home/AwardRecipientsRound12009/tabid/175/Default.aspx>

For this study, two technologies were utilised: Zotero, developed at George Mason in the Centre for History and New Media, and TAPoR, an older version of what is now Voyeur, developed by a group of Canadian researchers. These technologies were used to develop a new interface for the transcripts of trials at the Old Bailey in London. The Old Bailey records contain a wide and ongoing chronicle of trials and criminal processes, making them a riveting monument to the growth of attitudes, values, punishments, and the social history of crime.

Exercise B

Exploration of critical analysis of the project and develop a new project design by understanding the case study:

Case Study 1: Old Bailey Online

- Take from the Application Programming Interface (API) for "Old Bailey"
- Study a case study on "Zotero"
- Study a case study on feasibility and Voyant visualization

Case Study 2: "Erotics in Emily Dickinson"

- Watch the entire YouTube lecture
- <https://www.youtube.com/watch?v=3ZtM1t-xDKw>
- <https://open-video.org/details.php?videoid=8453> (Read)
- <https://ieeexplore.ieee.org/document/4119111/figures#figures> (Read)

Exercise C

- Engage in the process of addressing inquiries.
- Could you provide an analysis of the visualisation?
- What was the process for creating the visualisations?

Performing Text Analysis with VOYANT and Many Eyes

Text analysis methods are a subset of data mining. They rely on statistical analysis and algorithms that are capable of comprehending and processing characteristics of natural language in a meaningful manner. Visualisation technologies are employed to present a multitude of outcomes from text analysis and concurrently present their arguments. The upcoming lesson will shift its focus from "unstructured" texts to "structured" texts, which utilise markup to incorporate a layer of interpretation or analysis into the process.

A significant obstacle in data mining is the conversion of the findings into a readable format. Information visualisation condenses vast quantities of data into a visual representation that reveals patterns across multiple variables. The utilisation of visualisation tools for "reading" and analysing the outcomes of text mining presents several benefits and drawbacks. Attempt to discern how the rhetorical efficacy of the instruments operates inside the outcomes in this series of exercises.

Attainment of Outcomes

The learning outcomes include technical skills in data mining and text analysis, analytical skills, application knowledge, ethical awareness, and effective communication of findings. Doing text analysis and topic modelling with VOYANT.

Text analysis is a method used to do data mining on digitally encoded text files. One of the earliest manifestations of humanities computing, it is just a basic amalgamation of string search, matching, counting, and sorting functions that reveal word frequency, context, and lexical preferences. Topic modelling is a sophisticated method of text analysis that examines relationships, such as proximity, between textual elements and their frequency.

Works Cited and Recommended Texts

Flanders, Julia, and Fotis Jannidis. The Shape of Data in Digital Humanities : Modeling Texts and Text-Based Resources. Routledge, 2019.

Griffin, Gabriele. Research Methods for Reading Digital Data in the Digital Humanities. Edinburgh University Press, 2016.

Shalin Hai-Jew. Data Analytics in Digital Humanities. Springer, 2017.

Rahaman, V., Haider, A. (2021). Deconstructive Big Data Analytics: Literary Texts Analysis Through Atlas.ti Software. In: Sharma, S., Rahaman, V., Sinha, G.R. (eds) Big Data Analytics in Cognitive Social Media and Literary Texts. Springer, Singapore. https://doi.org/10.1007/978-981-16-4729-1_3

Rahaman, V., Agarwal, S. (2021). Necessity of Big Data Analytics in Social Media for Questioning the Existence and Survival of Women and the Marginalized People. In: Sharma, S., Rahaman, V., Sinha, G.R. (eds) Big Data Analytics in Cognitive Social Media and Literary Texts. Springer, Singapore. https://doi.org/10.1007/978-981-16-4729-1_7

CHAPTER ELEVEN

Teaching Digital Writing Authoring with TEI and Servigistics Arbortext Editor

TEI is geared towards researchers and scholars, requiring a deeper understanding of markup and digital text encoding. Arbortext is designed for technical writers and content developers, offering a range of tools for content creation, management, and publishing, such as Arbortext Editor and Arbortext Publisher. Both TEI and Arbortext are used for digital writing, and both are text and document management tools, catering to different audiences and purposes.

TEI and Arbortext for Critical, Creative and Content Writings

TEI focuses on preserving and analyzing scholarly texts, while Arbortext focuses on creating and managing technical documentation in industrial settings. The choice depends on project needs. TEI (Text Encoding Initiative) and Arbortext are both tools used in the realm of document creation and management, but they serve different purposes and operate in distinct contexts.

The Text Encoding Initiative (TEI) is a standard for digital text encoding, primarily used in academic and scholarly contexts to preserve and analyze literary, historical, and linguistic texts. Arbortext is a software suite for creating and managing technical documentation and publishing content, focusing on structured authoring and automated publishing processes. TEI uses XML-based markup to encode text, allowing for rich semantic structures and detailed annotations. Arbortext uses XML but is more focused on structured content for technical documents, supporting various data types and integrating with product lifecycle management systems. It provides a more rigid framework suited for technical documents, ensuring consistency and compliance with industry standards.

TEI and Arbortext:Collaboration and Integration

Collaboration

TEI Often collaborative but focused on scholarly projects, involving multiple stakeholders in the humanities. Arbortext Facilitates collaboration among technical teams, often integrating with other enterprise software for seamless workflows.

Integration

TEI Integrates with various digital humanities projects and platforms, but may not directly support industry-specific workflows. Arbortext has strong integration capabilities with PLM systems, content management systems (CMS), and other enterprise applications. The chapter is devided into three sections: TEI, Arbortext, and Creation of Content in Arbortext.

Text Encoding Initiatives (TEI) and similar standards are extensively discussed in academic literature, covering methodologies, applications, and case studies. Some notable articles and resources explore different dimensions of TEI initiatives, such as foundational articles, case studies, technical and methodological discussions, historical and theoretical perspectives, tool and software reviews, and advanced techniques. I prescribe the following texts to learn about the experiences of DH researchers:

- Lou Burnard's "The Text Encoding Initiative: A Guide"
- Susan Schreibman's "Text Encoding in the Digital Humanities"
- James Cummings's "The TEI Guidelines and the Digital Humanities: An Overview"
- Elena Pierazzo's "Encoding and Documenting Ancient Texts: The TEI Approach"
- David Greetham's "XML and TEI Encoding: Standards for Digital Texts"
- Gabriel Bodard's "TEI for Scholars: A Practical Guide to Encoding"
- Julia Flanders' "The Historical Development of Text Encoding Standards"

The Text Encoding Initiative (TEI) is a long-standing project in the Digital Humanities, providing guidelines for the creation and management of digital data created and used by researchers in the Humanities. TEI XML focuses on the meaning of text rather than its appearance, is independent of any particular software environment, and was designed by and for the scholarly research community. It offers advantages such as focusing on meaning before format, software independence, and ensuring that textual resources can be easily shared and adapted between different software environments. However, true interoperability remains problematic within the same software style.

The TEI XML document represents a text without any special magic, and its content represents what its creator considers significant about its structure and content. The TEI was first developed over thirty years ago as a research project in the field of "humanities computing" to create machine-readable textual resources. The TEI evolves by responding to changes considered beneficial by its user community while ignoring those not. The TEI community is diverse and open, with expertise in most humanities disciplines. This chapter aims to showcase various TEI markup varieties, aiming to be accessible to a wide readership, including digital humanists and those not yet fully embracing the computer. The TEI framework emphasizes the continuity of all types of documents, including digital, printed, and manuscript forms. It treats all digital documents the same, regardless of their digital origin. TEI documents use XML, a widely used formal encoding language, to represent structured data and label parts with named tags. The TEI's Guidelines are freely accessible at <http://www.tei-c.org/Guidelines>.

Introduction

Teaching text encoding initiatives teaches students how to encode, structure, and annotate text data for digital preservation, linguistic analysis, and information retrieval. Key learning outcomes include an introduction to text encoding, an overview of TEI and other standards, encoding text data, practical application, text analysis and retrieval, advanced topics in schema design and customization, interoperability and data integration, ethical considerations, best practices, documentation, and communication. The outcomes include technical skills, analytical skills, practical experience, ethical awareness, and communication skills. This approach prepares students to work effectively with encoded texts and contribute to fields like digital humanities, linguistics, and information science. Elena Pierazzo's "Textual Scholarship and Text Encoding" explores the role of text encoding in digital editing theory and its impact on editor workflow. It compares the evolution of editors as encoders and the demand for new tools, questioning traditional roles. Julia Flanders & Fotis Jannidis edited volume *The Shape of Data in Digital Humanities Modeling Texts and Text-based Resources* discusses the role of data modelling in digital humanities, focusing on topics such as orientation, data modelling in a Digital Humanities context, topics in Digital Humanities data modelling, how modelling standards evolve: the case of the TEI, how subjective is your model?, modelling space in historical texts, modelling time, visualizing information, ontologies and data modelling. The authors also discuss the evolution of modelling standards, the subjective nature of models, and the role of modelling in the humanities.

Using text encoding initiatives involves applying standardized methods to structure and represent text data digitally. These initiatives, such as the Text Encoding Initiative (TEI), provide guidelines for encoding texts in a way that preserves their scholarly value and ensures interoperability between different systems. Follow to use text encoding initiatives effectively:

1. Understanding the Basics

1.1. Learn the Standards

Text Encoding Initiative (TEI): Familiarize yourself with TEI guidelines, which offer a comprehensive framework for encoding literary and historical texts. Review the TEI P5 guidelines available on the TEI website.

Other Standards: Understand other relevant standards, such as XML (eXtensible Markup Language), which is often used in conjunction with TEI.

1.2. Get the Tools

- Text Editors: Use text editors that support XML, such as Oxygen XML Editor, Notepad++, or Visual Studio Code.
- Validation Tools: Use tools like XML Schema Validators and TEI validation tools to check the correctness of your encoded texts.

2. Preparing Your Text

2.1. Text Selection and Preparation

- Select Texts: Choose the texts you want to encode. Ensure they are well-organized and in a format that can be easily converted to XML.
- Clean and Preprocess: Clean the text for encoding by removing any irrelevant information or formatting issues.

2.2. Define Encoding Goals

- Purpose: Determine the purpose of encoding, such as preserving textual integrity, facilitating scholarly analysis, or improving accessibility.
- Scope: Decide the scope of encoding, including what elements and features of the text will be represented.

3. Encoding the Text

3.1. Create an XML Document

- Structure: Start with a basic XML document structure. Define the root element, typically <TEI>, and include necessary namespaces and attributes.
- Basic Elements: Add basic TEI elements such as <teiHeader>, <text>, and <body>, according to the TEI guidelines.

3.2. Apply TEI Guidelines

- Tagging: Use TEI tags to encode various elements of the text, including:
- Metadata: Metadata about the text, such as the title, author, and publication details, using <teiHeader>.
- Text Structure: Structure of the text, such as chapters, sections, and paragraphs, using tags like <div>, <p>, and <head>.
- Annotations: Add annotations, notes, and comments using tags like <note>, <bibl>, and <ref>.
- Attributes: Use attributes to provide additional information or context, such as <title type="main"> or <person role="author">.

4. Validation and Quality Assurance

4.1. Validate the XML

- Schema Validation: Use XML schema validators to ensure that your XML document adheres to the TEI schema.
- TEI Validation: Utilize TEI-specific validation tools to check for compliance with TEI guidelines.

4.2. Review and Refine

- Proofreading: Manually review the encoded text to ensure accuracy and completeness.
- Feedback: Seek feedback from peers or experts to improve the encoding quality.

5. Using Encoded Texts

5.1. Text Analysis

- Use tools and languages like XPath and XQuery to extract and analyze specific data from the encoded text.
- Create visual representations of the data using tools such as Voyant Tools or custom visualization scripts.

5.2. Interoperability

- Ensure that the encoded text can be integrated with other systems or databases, supporting data interoperability and sharing.
- Publish encoded texts on platforms that support TEI or other standards, ensuring broad accessibility and usability.

6. Documenting and Sharing

6.1. Documentation

Documentation is a crucial tool in various fields, serving as a formal record of work, decisions, and outcomes. It supports knowledge sharing, compliance, and accountability, and streamlines operations. Documentation can be technical, research, educational, project, or creative. Best practices include clarity, precision, consistency, comprehensiveness, accessibility, version control, review, and validation. Documentation processes include gathering data, organizing it, creating documents, editing and revising, sharing, and maintaining. By adhering to best practices and focusing on clarity, consistency, and accessibility, organizations can enhance the value and impact of their documentation, contributing to the broader body of knowledge and innovation.

6.2. Sharing and Collaboration

- Repositories: Share encoded texts through repositories or databases that support text encoding standards.
- Collaboration: Collaborate with other researchers or institutions to improve and expand the encoded data.

7. Ethical and Practical Considerations

7.1. Ethical Issues

- Privacy: Ensure that the encoding process respects privacy and copyright issues.
- Integrity: Maintain the integrity of the text and avoid misrepresentation during encoding.

7.2. Best Practices

Follow best practices for consistency in encoding and documentation, and regularly update encoded texts for accuracy and relevance. Utilize text encoding initiatives to preserve, analyze, and communicate textual information in digital formats.

Outcomes of Study

Teaching the Text Encoding Initiative (TEI) can be a complex but highly rewarding endeavour. The TEI provides guidelines for encoding texts in a machine-readable format, which is crucial for digital humanities research, archiving, and scholarly communication. When teaching TEI, there are several key learning outcomes that educators typically aim for:

1. **Understanding of TEI Basics**: Students should gain a foundational understanding of what TEI is, including its history, purpose, and how it fits into the broader field of digital humanities. This includes familiarization with TEI's role in encoding texts to preserve their structure and content.
2. **Proficiency in TEI Encoding**: Learners should be able to apply TEI guidelines to encode a variety of texts. This includes understanding the TEI XML schema, using TEI elements and attributes, and employing encoding practices to represent different text features like headings, paragraphs, annotations, and metadata.
3. **Application of TEI in Different Contexts**: Students should learn how TEI can be applied to various types of texts and projects, such as literary works, historical documents, or scholarly editions. This might involve encoding primary source materials or creating digital editions of texts.
4. **Evaluation and Critique of TEI Projects**: Learners should develop the ability to assess the quality and effectiveness of TEI-encoded texts and projects. This includes evaluating the accuracy of the encoding, the comprehensiveness of metadata, and the overall usability of the digital representation.
5. **Integration with Other Tools and Standards**: Understanding how TEI interacts with other digital tools and standards, such as other XML-based schemas, content management systems, and digital repositories, is crucial. This helps students see the bigger picture of how TEI fits into digital workflows and ecosystems.
6. **Hands-On Experience**: Practical experience is essential. Students should be able to work with TEI tools, such as editors (like Oxygen XML Editor), validation tools, and converters. This hands-on practice helps solidify theoretical knowledge and develops technical skills.
7. Critical Thinking and Problem-Solving: Teaching TEI should foster critical thinking about how to best represent different types of textual information and how to handle ambiguities or challenges in text encoding. Students should be able to troubleshoot issues that arise

during the encoding process.

8. **Awareness of TEI Community and Resources**: Students should be aware of the TEI community, including its forums, conferences, and other resources. This knowledge helps learners stay current with developments in the field and connect with other professionals and scholars.

By achieving these outcomes, students will be well-prepared to use TEI in their projects and contribute to the broader digital text encoding and digital humanities field.

Writing and Publishing with Servigistics Arbortext Editor

Arbortext is a software suite for creating, managing, and publishing technical documentation, particularly in industries like aerospace, defense, and manufacturing. It supports XML and SGML documents, offers content management tools, and allows easy publishing in various formats. It can integrate with content management systems, supports templates and customization, and includes validation tools. Arbortext is suitable for creating technical manuals, compliance documentation, and multilingual publishing, making it a powerful tool for organizations producing high-quality, structured technical content efficiently.

PTC University provides training and educational resources for Arbortext users, including courses, tutorials, and certification programs. They also offer documentation and support resources, foster a user community, and keep users informed about updates and innovations. This connection ensures that Arbortext users have access to the necessary training and resources to maximize its capabilities in their documentation processes.

The section provides an introduction to editing and authoring with Servigistics Arbortext Editor, including examples and step-by-step exercises. It requires familiarity with operating systems and computer skills. Exercises cover DocBook and DITA (Darwin Information Typing Architecture) document types, highlighting differences in features:

- Servigistics Arbortext Architect

- Servigistics Arbortext Styler
- Servigistics Arbortext Publishing Engine

In XML and HTML, structured documents adhere to a set of guidelines known as a "document type". The guidelines that apply to these papers are known as "document types." Only content that complies with these guidelines is permitted to be added to documents using Servigistics Arbortext Editor. Tags, attributes, and tag structure are examples of document kinds. Structured documents are mostly made up of tags, with attributes adding more details. All other tags defined in the document type are contained in a single tag that is unique to each document type. The tag hierarchy and whether a tag is necessary or optional are also specified by the document type. Every document type has a stylesheet attached to it that uses style parameters to regulate how the document looks. In other words, Structured documents follow a set of rules called a "document type" in XML and HTML. These documents are governed by a set of rules called "document types." In Servigistics Arbortext Editor, the editor checks these rules and only allows content to be inserted into the document that conforms to them. Document types include tags, attributes, and the structure of tags. Tags are the basic building blocks of structured documents, with attributes providing additional information. Each document type has a single tag that contains all other tags defined in the document type. The document type also defines the tag hierarchy and whether a tag is optional or required. Stylesheets are associated with each document type, controlling the appearance of the document through style settings. These settings can include basic formatting information like font size, paragraph spacing, and page layout, or more advanced formatting like automatic generation of a table of contents and an index.

The Servigistics Arbortext Editor Environment

Servigistics Arbortext Editor follows standard Windows conventions, offering features like opening samples, viewing cursor changes, expanding and collapsing tag content, using drag and drop, and viewing generated text.

Opening a Sample Document

Start Servigistics Arbortext Editor.

Many document types in Servigistics Arbortext Editor keep a template and sample document in terms of them. A template is a predefined set of empty tags that give all of the basic tagging required for a document. Here, learn how to open a sample document.

1. Choose File > New to open the New Document dialog box.

2. Choose DocBook in the Category list and Arbortext XML DocBook V4.0 in the Type list, then select the Sample option and click OK.

The sample document displays in the Servigistics Arbortext Editor window. It must be noted that the sample document that displays in your Servigistics Arbortext Editor window differs from the document shown in the following examples.

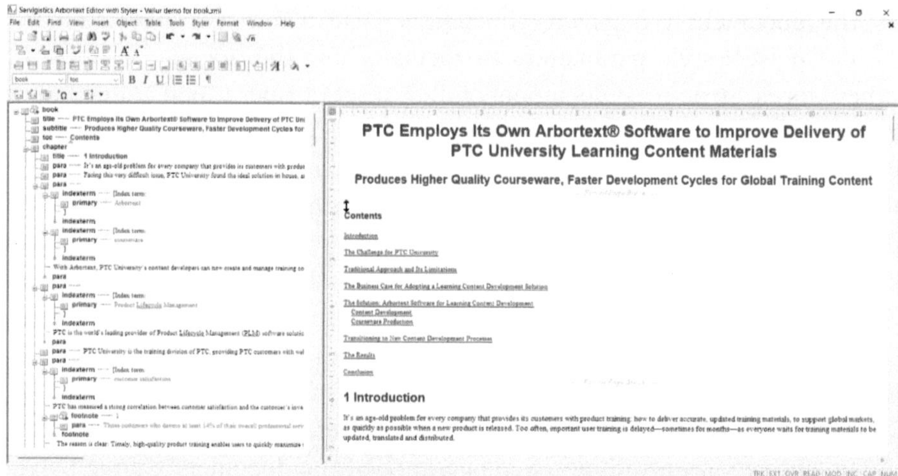

Figure1: Sample Document

Menus and Toolbars

The menus and toolbars display a standard set of commands. For detailed descriptions of the menus, toolbars, and their functionality, refer to the online Help topics available from Help > Servigistics Arbortext Editor.

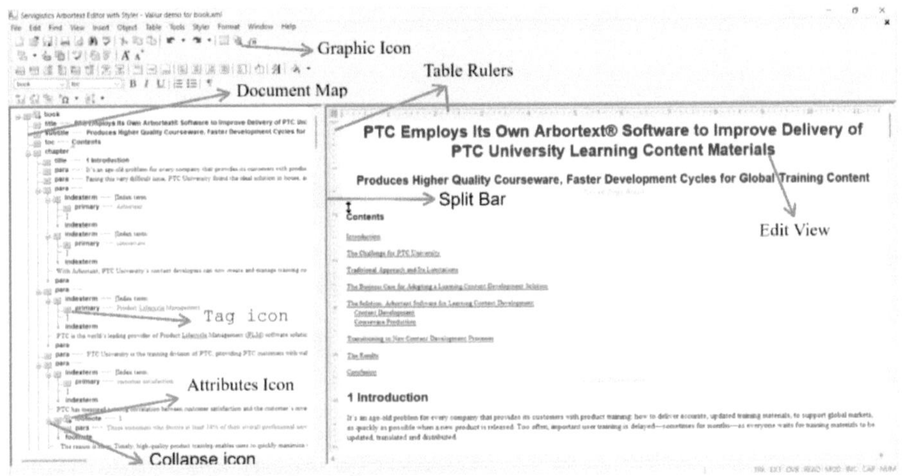

Figure 2: Various Icons in the Interface

Edit View

The Edit view displays your document with its content and the tags that control the structure of the document. You can change the display of these tags using the View menu. The options enable you to control how much of the tagging structure you want to see as you add content and new tags to your document.

- *Full Tags* — Displays tag icons and names.
- *No Tags* — Suppresses the display of tags.

If you are accustomed to working in a "tagged view" environment (for example, with HTML documents), you might want to work with the tags displayed in Servigistics Arbortext Editor.

Document Map

The Document Map enables you to navigate a graphical outline of the document structure. You can also collapse large sections of the document and move them within the Document Map. The Document Map and the Edit view are fully interactive, so any changes made in one pane are immediately reflected in the other. The following figure shows the Document Map components.

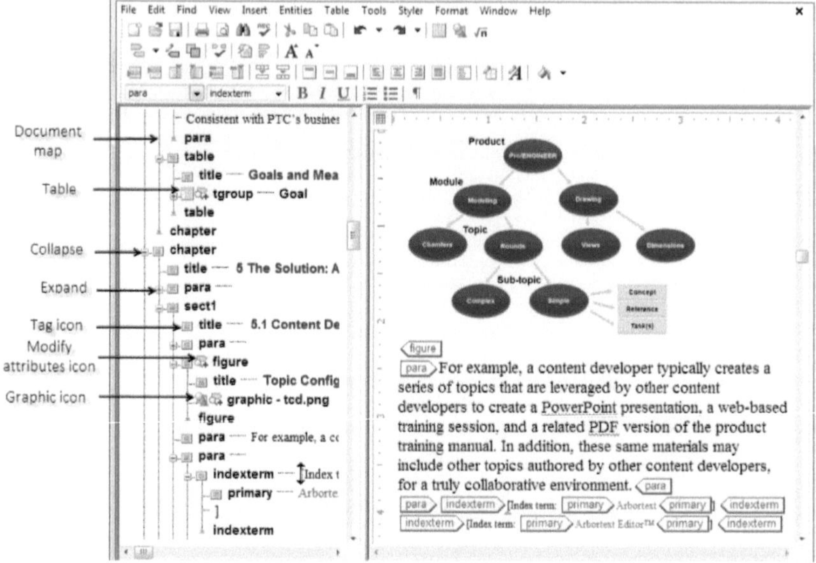

Figure 4: Document Map

Creating a New Document

Steps to create a new document:

1. Choose File > New. See the New Document dialog box opens.

2. In the New Document dialog box, select DocBook in the Category list and Arbortext XML DocBook V4.0 in the Type list and then click OK.

An Arbortext XML DocBook template is already there into the Servigistics Arbortext Editor window. The template keeps tags that are pre-populated in your document. User's template may differ slightly from the template used in this chapter.

3. Save your document by choosing File > Save. See the Save As dialog box opens.

4. In the File Name field, *type mydocument.*

5. Navigate to the folder where you want to save the document and *click Save.*

By default, Servigistics Arbortext Editor saves new documents in the directory that was last used. Servigistics Arbortext Editor saves your new document in the folder you selected.

Viewing Cursor Changes

After opening Arbortext XML DocBook V4.0 sample document in Servigistics Arbortext Editor. Yoy see the Servigistics Arbortext Editor cursor alters appearance based on the location of the cursor in the Document Map and Edit view. The following steps view some of the cursor changes:

1. Use the arrow keys to navigate through the Document Map. The cursor will change its shape depending on its location.

2. Move the cursor to the left of a para tag. The *I-beam cursor* indicates that you can enter text and possibly other tags.

3. Type the following text: Inserting text into my document using the Document Map. As you type, a new para tag is added automatically to accommodate the new text.

4. Move the cursor to the end of a chapter tag. The cursor appears as a double-headed arrow indicating that no text insertion is allowed at this location.

5. Type your name. A message will appear on the status bar, warning you that inserting text is not allowed.

6. Click outside of the Servigistics Arbortext Editor window.

The cursor changes to the inactive cursor showing inactive window.

Expanding and Collapsing Tag Content

Using the Document Map, a user views or hides the content of tags to make it easier to navigate through your document. Follow these steps to collapse and expand tag content:

1. Find the book tag at the top of the Document Map. The above figure shows the completely expanded hierarchy of document tag.

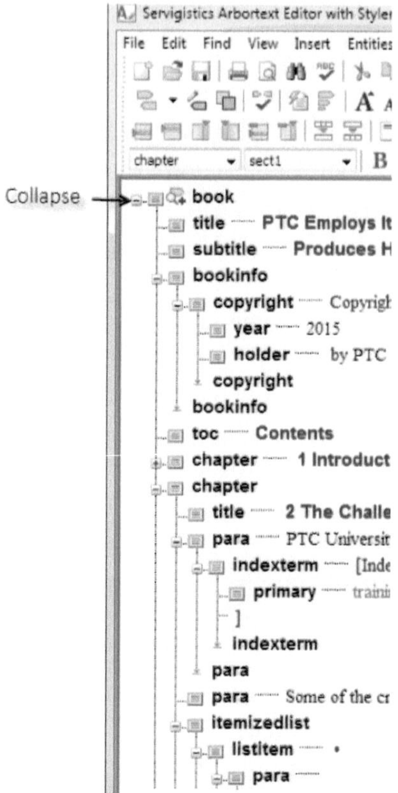

Figure 6: Collapse Document Map

2. Click the collapse icon to the left of the book element. It must be noted that the entire document content collapses, but the title remains so you can identify the collapsed content. The collapse icon is replaced with the expand icon , as in the following figure.

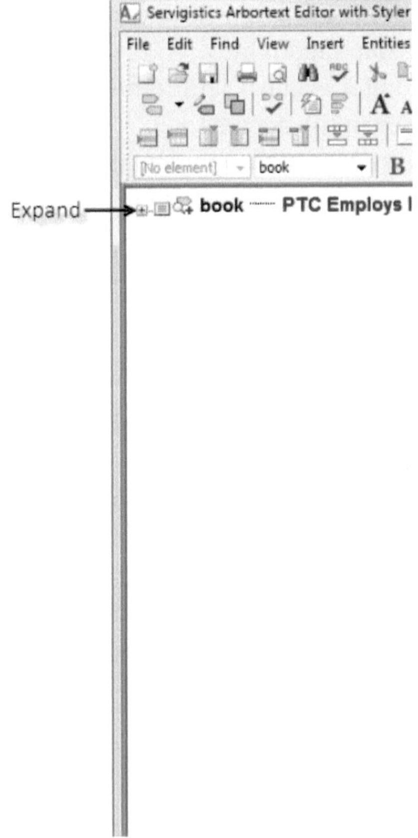

Figure 7: Expand Document Map

Using Drag and Drop

You can drag and drop just content, a tag with its content, an empty tag, or a mix of content and tags. You can use drag and drop in the following locations:

- Within a document
- Between different views of a document in the same Editor window
- Between separate documents
- Between applications

Follow these steps to use drag and drop:

3. Click and, holding down the mouse button, drag the selected text down the Document Map hierarchy.

Notice how the pointer changes represented by symbols.

4. Move your cursor in the document.

5. Release the mouse button to complete the drop operation.

Select text within a **para tag** and drag it to another location in the document, using the same symbols as when moving a tag and its content. The same symbols are displayed for this operation.

Deleting Tags, Content and Undo

You can delete either just text or a tag with its content. Follow these steps to delete a tag:

1. In the Document Map, click the tag icon to the left of a para element.

2. Press the DELETE key.

The element and its contents are deleted.

3. Click the Undo toolbar button to undo the deletion.

You could also select some of the text inside of the para tag and delete in the same way.

Get Generated Text

Generated text is defined and automatically inserted in your document according to your document type's stylesheet. Examples of generated text include a table of contents, an index, and list numbers. Generated text is displayed in a different font color (blue by default) and cannot be edited directly in Servigistics Arbortext Editor. Follow these steps to change the display of generated text:

1. Choose Tools > Preferences and select the **Window** category.

2. If **Full Menus** is not checked, click on the check box. Click OK.

3. Choose View > Generated Text > **Show** to clear the selection and suppress the display of generated text.

4. Scroll through your document and note the absence of bullets, chapter numbers, and list numbers.

5. Choose View > Generated Text > **Show** again to restore the display of generated text.

6. Choose View > Generated Text and note the choices available for updating generated text. Verify that the Partial Auto-Updates option is selected.

7. Press the ESC key to exit from the menu.

Let's Arbortext: Creating a New Document

Understand first thing first that structured documents follow a set of rules called a "document type" and are governed by XML and HTML. These documents have tags, attributes, and a structure for arranging them. Document types like DocBook and DITA (Darwin Information Typing Architecture) define the tags, their hierarchy, and their arrangement. Stylesheets are used to control the appearance of these documents, ranging from basic formatting to advanced features like table of contents and index generation.

Arbortext XML DocBook Template

To create a new document in Arbortext, launch the Arbortext Editor application, select a document type (XML, SGML), set necessary properties, add content, use templates, validate against DTDs or schemas, save your work, preview and print, and export in PDF or HTML formats. To speed up your workflow, familiarize yourself with keyboard shortcuts, use Arbortext's extensive documentation and help resources, and keep regular backups to avoid losing progress. Regular validation against DTDs or schemas helps catch errors. Save your work frequently, preview and print, and export in various formats.

Follow these steps to create a new document:

1. Choose File > New.

The New Document dialog box opens.

2. In the New Document dialog box, select DocBook in the Category list and Arbortext XML DocBook V4.0 in the Type list and then click OK.

An Arbortext XML DocBook template is loaded into the Servigistics Arbortext Editor window. The template includes tags that are pre-populated in your document. Your template may differ slightly from the template used in this book.

3. Save your document by choosing File > Save.

The Save As dialog box opens.

4. In the File Name field, type mydocument.

5. Navigate to the folder where you want to save the document and click Save.

By default, Servigistics Arbortext Editor saves new documents in the directory that was last used. Servigistics Arbortext Editor saves new document in the folder you selected.

Let's follow more simple steps in bullets for creating a new document in Arbortext

• Open Arbortext Editor: Launch the application on your computer.

• Create a New Document: Go to File > New or press Ctrl + N.

• Select Document Type: Choose the appropriate document type based on your project requirements.

• Set Document Properties: Set necessary properties, including metadata.

• Add Content: Add content using the editor, either typing directly or importing existing text.

• Use Templates: Apply templates to ensure consistency.

• Validate Document: Regularly validate your document against the DTD or schema.

• Save Your Document: Save your work frequently.

• Preview and Print: Use View options to preview or print your document.

• Export: Export your document in various formats (e.g., PDF, HTML, ePUB).

For fast working culture follow and learn keyboard shortcuts, use Help Documentation, and keep never forget to keep regular backups.

Tags and Content Insertion

This exercise demonstrates how to insert tags and content in an Arbortext XML DocBook document. To use the Quick Tags feature, start at the beginning of a paragraph, press ENTER, and click on "para" to insert a new tag. Mastering these techniques will improve document efficiency and quality.

Arbortext XML DocBook allows for tag insertion using the Insert Markup dialog box and toolbar button. The Quick Tags feature is used to insert tags, and the cursor is automatically positioned for text input. To insert text in a new paragraph, place the cursor in the Edit view and choose

View > Full Tags. In the Edit view, place the cursor between title tags and type "Creating Structured Documents." Insert new elements between the next set of title tags. Structured documents allow authors to focus on content. To select tags from the Quick Tags list, press ENTER. To insert a note element, click on "note" and type "This document was written to demonstrate entering content into a structured document." Save your changes by choosing File > Save.

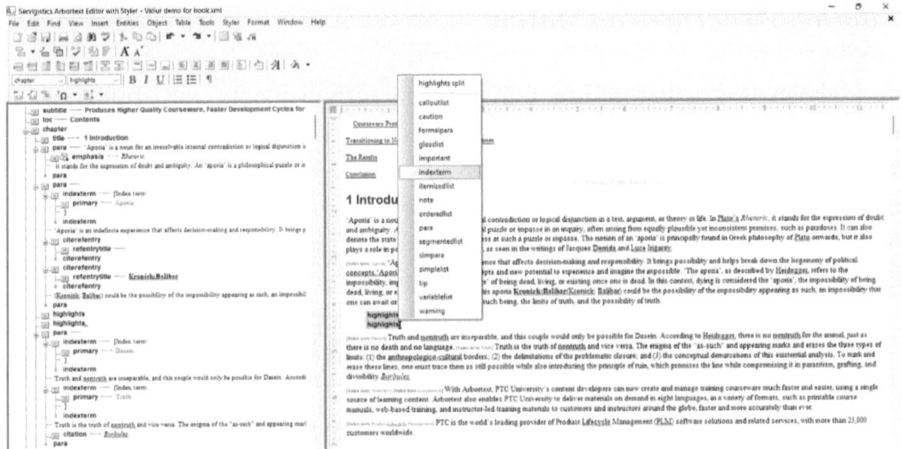

Figure 12: **Pop up of Quick Tags**

Insert tags and content into your new document following the steps given below:

1. In the **Document Map**, place your cursor at the beginning of an existing paragraph.

2. Press ENTER to display the **Quick Tags** (see the figure above) menu.

It is important to understand that only the **tags** that the document type allows at that location are available.

3. Using the mouse, click on **para** to insert a new para tag.

The cursor is positioned for inserting text automatically.

4. Type Inserting text in a new paragraph.

5. Place the cursor in the Edit view and choose View > Full Tags.

6. In the **Edit** view, place the cursor between the title tags at the top of the document and type **Creating Structured Documents**

7. Place the cursor between the next set of title **tags** (under the chapter tag) and type **Inserting New Elements**.

8. Between the second set of para tags, type deconstruction is a literary study of history.

9. Press ENTER to select tags from the Quick Tags list.

10. Click on note to insert a note element

11. Type *Teaching humanities to become humanities scientists is the first book on digital humanities pedagogies in India.*

12. Choose File > Save to save your changes.

Adding Structure to Content

Servigistics Arbortext Editor converts paragraph blocks into bulleted or numbered lists. It generates a numeric list with step-by-step instructions and appropriate indentation. The process reduces manual formatting and ensures consistent presentation. Servigistics Arbortext Editor enables you to convert blocks of paragraphs into bulleted or numbered lists. Steps to create a numbered list:

1. Position your cursor to the right of the last para tag.

2. Insert a new para tag into your document by pressing ENTER and selecting the para tag from the **Quick Tags** list.

3. Enter the following text, inserting a new para tag at the end of each the first three lines, resulting in four para elements and their content:

- A numeric list can provide step by step instructions.
- Each item is preceded by a number, which is automatically generated by Servigistics Arbortext Editor.
- The appropriate indentation is also determined and applied automatically.
- Working with structured content reduces the amount of manually applied formatting required for consistent presentation.

4. Select all four paragraphs (including the para tags) and click on the Numeric List toolbar button on the Application toolbar.

The four paragraphs are displayed as a numeric list. You can also develop a list by inserting an numeric or bullet list tag into your document and adding list items to the list.

Creating and Inserting a Text Entity

Entities are blocks of content that can be reused repeatedly in documents. They can be created as file or text entities, and can be displayed using an icon or expanded content. Full menus are available for entities. DITA (Darwin Information Typing Architecture) documents reuse content differently.

There are several menus and options, such as the Entities menu, that are only available if you have elected to display full menus. To display full menus, choose Tools > Preferences, select the Window tab, and click the check box next to Full Menus. Click OK to exit from the Preferences dialog box.

Steps to create and insert a text entity are given below:

1. Select a range of text.
2. Choose Entities > Create Text Entity From Selection.

The Create Text Entity from Selection dialog box opens.

3. In the Name field, type mytext and click OK to close the dialog box.
4. Place your cursor within a para tag and choose Entities > Text.

The Text Entities dialog box opens.

5. Select the mytext text entity.
6. Click Insert, then click Close to close the dialog box.

The text entity is inserted as an icon.

7. Choose View > Text Entity to view the expanded content of the entity.

Inserting Links

Let's know how to insert links in Arbortext XML DocBook documents using Link tags. The process involves inserting a new para tag, selecting the URL, and clicking Insert. For this exercise, use the Arbortext XML DocBook document you modified in the previous exercise. User can link from one location in your document to another, or to a URL, using Link tags.

Follow these steps to insert a link to a URL:

1. Insert a new **para** tag.

2. Type *For more information about structured documentation, refer to the HITS website.*

3. Select *the words HITS website, and choose* Insert > **Link.**

The Insert Link dialog box opens.

4. Choose the Web tab, type http://www.hitslab.in/ in the URL field, and click Insert to insert the link and close the dialog box.

5. Double-click on the highlighted link to open your web browser and display the HITS web site.

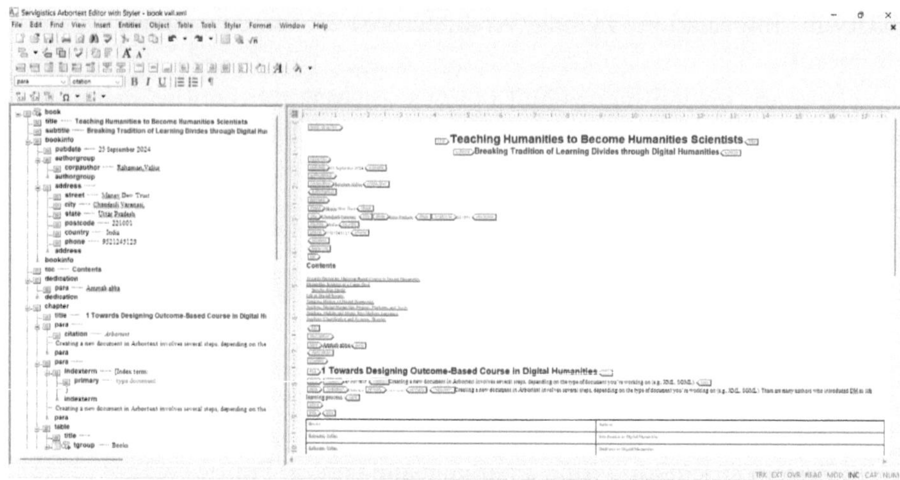

Figure 13: XML view of Insertion of Content in Arbortext

Modifying Attributes

This exercise uses the Arbortext XML DocBook document, where attributes define tags and assign properties like file references, magnification, and font styles. A document's structure includes tags like sections, titles, paragraphs, and lists. Attributes define specific aspects of these tags, assigning properties like file references, magnification, and font styles. To modify attributes, select a word, apply emphasis, and modify attributes.

Step to modify and attribute to change a font style following the istructions:

1. Select any single word within a paragraph and press ENTER to activate the Quick Tags menu.

2. Select the emphasis tag.

The word formatting changes to italics. Italics is the default font style when emphasis is applied to text in this document type.

3. Choose Edit > Modify Attributes.

The Modify Attributes dialog box opens.

4. Type bold in the role field and click OK to close the dialog box.

Notice that the formatting for the word changes from italics to bold in the Edit view and the Document Map.

5. In the Document Map, click on the corresponding Modify Attributes icon to see the list of attributes that have been defined for this tag.

6. Click on the Modify Attributes icon again to close the list of attributes.

Insert Graphics and Symbols

This exercise demonstrates how to insert graphics in Servigistics Arbortext Editor. The process involves inserting a new para tag, selecting Insert > Graphic, choosing an inlinegraphic tag, locating the graphic file, importing the graphic, modifying attributes, and scaling the graphic to 25 percent of its original size.

Follow these steps to insert a graphic and modify the size of the graphic:

1. Insert a new para tag.

2. Choose Insert > Graphic.

The Insert Graphic dialog box opens.

3. Choose the inlinegraphic tag to allow your graphic to remain in line with the flow of text in your document and click OK.

The ***Locate Graphic*** *file to reference dialog box opens.*

4. Navigate to a graphic file on your system, or open the graphics folder in the Servigistics Arbortext Editor installation folder and select instrument.jpg, then select Open to insert the graphic.

See the **graphic** is inserted in your document in existing text.

5. Display the attributes associated with your new graphic by clicking on the Modify Attributes icon in the Document Map.

6. Click once on the displayed attributes to open the Modify Attributes dialog box.

7. Type 25 in the scale field and click OK to close the dialog box. The graphic is scaled to 25 percent of its original size.

For insertion of symbols, use the Arbortext XML DocBook document you modified in the previous exercise.

You can insert a variety of symbols into your document. Follow these steps to insert a symbol:

1. Place your cursor within a para tag.

2. Choose Insert > Symbol.

The Insert Symbol dialog box displays.

3. Click on a symbol in the dialog box.

4. Click Insert to insert the symbol at the cursor location.
5. Click Close to close the dialog box.

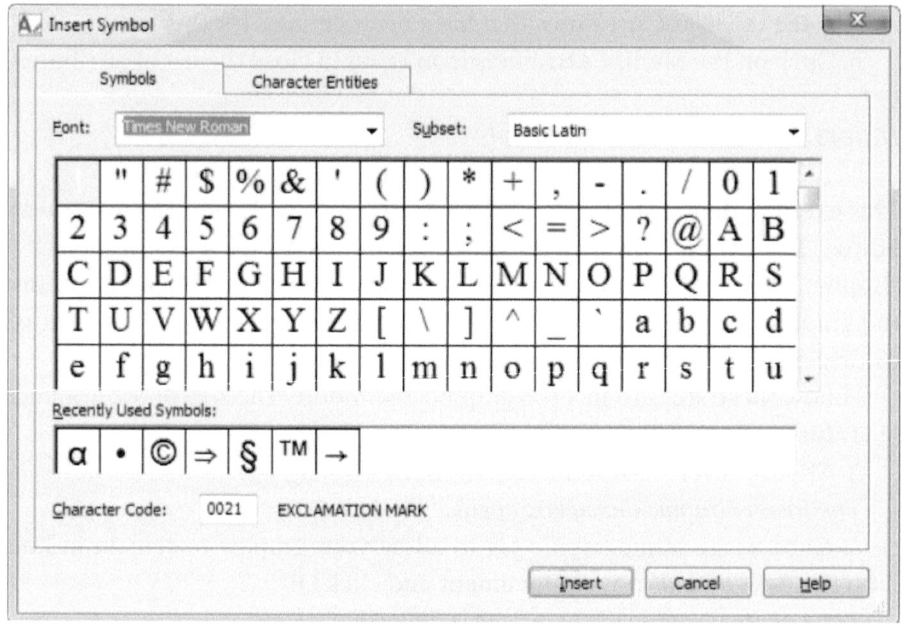

Figure 14:Insert Symbols with Symbol dialog box

Searching for Contents, Tags, and Tables

Servigistics Arbortext Editor offers a standard find and replace feature, allowing users to search for content in a document by selecting Find > Find/ Replace, and selecting the Match Whole Word Only checkbox.

Steps to find content in a document are given below:

1. Choose Find > Find/Replace.

The Find/Replace dialog box displays.

2. Type structure in the Find What field.
3. Click the Find Next button.

The first occurrence of a word containing structure is highlighted in user's document. If user intends to search just for the word "structure," user can select the Match Whole Word Only check box before searching for the word.

4. Click Cancel to close the dialog box.

To find tags in a document, select Find > Find Tag/Attribute, type inlinegraphic in Tag Name, click Find Next, search for specific attribute or value, and click Cancel.

To find tags in a document, select Find > Find Tag/Attribute, type inlinegraphic in Tag Name, click Find Next, search for specific attribute or value, and click Cancel. Steps to find a tag in a document are given below:

1. Choose Find > Find Tag/Attribute.

The Find Tag/Attribute dialog box displays.

2. Type inlinegraphic in the Tag Name field.

3. Click the Find Next button.

The first occurrence of an inlinegraphic tag is highlighted in your document. You can also search for a tag with a specific attribute or attribute value.

4. Click Cancel to close the dialog box.

Servigistics Arbortext Editor is also a table editor that allows users to author tables, manipulate their parts in the Edit view, and insert new columns. To use the editor, place the cursor inside a para tag, choose **Insert > Table**, increase the number of rows, select a column, apply cell shading, and deselect the column.

Servigistics Arbortext Editor provides a table editor to assist you with authoring tables. The table editor hides the tags associated with a table and enables you to manipulate the parts of a table in the Edit view.

Follow these steps to insert and work with a table in your document:

1. Place your cursor inside a para tag.

2. Choose Insert > Table.

The Insert Table dialog box opens.

3. In the Rows field, click the up arrow to increase the number of rows to 7, then click OK.

The table is inserted into your document.

4. Place the cursor in the first cell in the table.

5. Click on the Insert Column Left toolbar button.

A new column is inserted into the table to the left of the cursor. You can also choose Table > Insert > Column Left for this and other table operations.

6. Select the new column by clicking in the column ruler above the column.

The cursor changes to a down arrow when it is in the ruler:

7. Click on the Span Cells toolbar button .

All of the cells in the column are joined together.

8. Click the arrow on the Apply Cell Shading toolbar button to display a drop down list.

9. Select a color from the color palette.

10. Click in another area of the table to deselect the column to view the cell shading.

Also remember, Servigistics Arbortext Editor automatically checks your document for spelling errors as you type, marking any suspect words with a red wavy line. It also automatically corrects a limited set of misspelled words and similar errors. You can also explicitly check a selected portion of a document or the entire document for spelling errors. To check spelling, follow these steps:

1. Choose Tools > Preferences.
2. Select the Spelling category icon.
3. Make sure the Check Spelling as you type spelling preference is on and click OK.
4. Place your cursor in a para tag and enter the misspelled word bok.
5. Right-click on the misspelled word to get a shortcut menu with alternative words.
6. Choose book from the menu.
7. Enter another misspelled word in the para tag and select the contents.
8. Choose Tools > Spelling.
9. From the list of Suggestions, click on the correct word and choose Change to correct the misspelled word.
10. Close the status message and the Spelling dialog box.

Publish Document

After creating a structured docuemnt of a book. One can publish the document for Web, EPUB, HTML, PDF, RTF and other language formats easily. See the figure below:

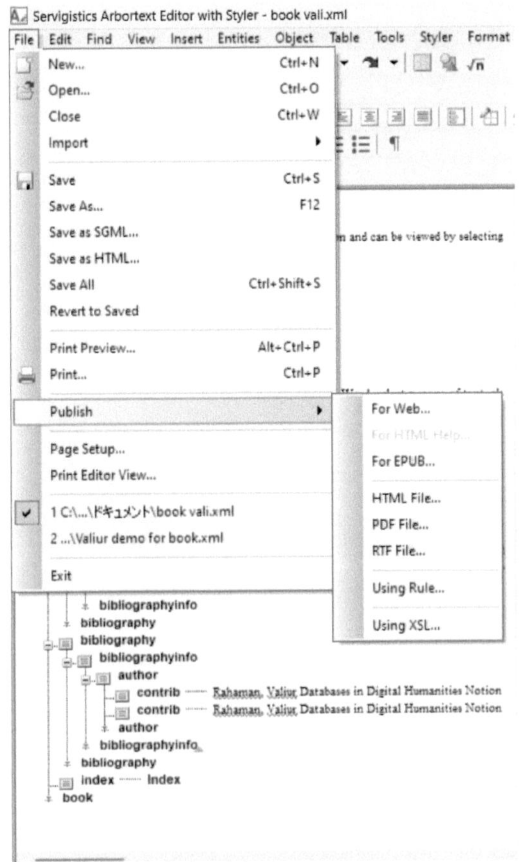

Figure 15:Publication the Final Stage

You get an output as a hypertext book:

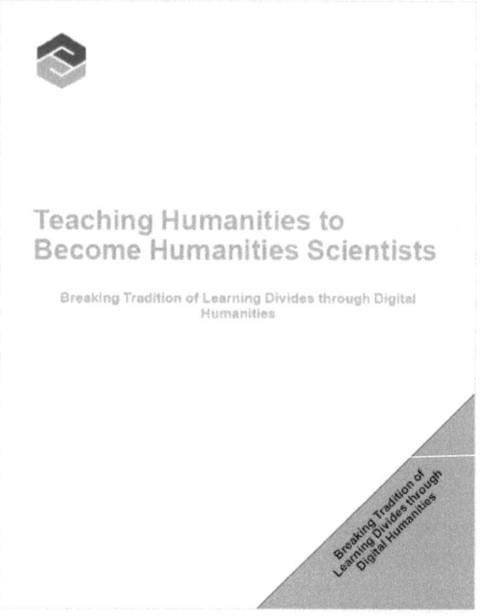

Figure 16 :Output of inserted information in the first stuctured document template

Saving Document as SGML/HTML

Servigistics Arbortext Editor also allows document saving as an HTML file, displaying in a web browser, not available for DITA (Darwin Information Typing Architecture) documents. Saves file, opens in browser, and creates graphics folder.

Contact the author for an intensive teacher training/FDP on TEI/ ARBORTEXT/Students' placement training/expert lecture at <valiur.bsb@gmail.com>.

Works Cited and Recommended Readings

Burnard, Lou. *What Is the Text Encoding Initiative?*. OpenEdition Press, 2014, https://doi.org/10.4000/books.oep.426.

Bradley, N. *The XML Companion. Reading*, MA: Addison-Wesley. 2001.

Carlson, G. Literary Works in Machine-Readable Form. Computers and the Humanities 1: 75–102. 1967. “Electronic Textual Editing: Authorial Translation: The Case of Samuel Beckett’s Stirrings Still / Soubresauts [Dirk van Hulle, University of Antwerp, Belgium].” TEI, tei-c.org/Vault/ETE/Preview/vanhulle.html#body.1_div.2. Accessed 9 Sept. 2024.

Cummings, J. "The TEI Guidelines and the Digital Humanities: An Overview"

Cummings, J. "The Text Encoding Initiative and the Study of Literature". In *A Companion to Digital Literary Studies*, ed. Ray Siemens, Susan Schreibman. Oxford: Blackwell, 2008. <https://companions.digitalhumanities.org/DLS/>

Flanders, J. *Shape of data in digital humanities: Modeling texts and text-based resources.* NY: Routledge. 2020.

Get Started with Arbortext Editor. PTC University. <https://learningconnector.ptc.com/playlist/PL1651639068422/get-started-with-arbortext-editor>.

Hockey, Susan. Electronic Texts in the Humanities. Oxford: Oxford University Press. 2000.

Ide, Nancy, and Jean Véronis. Text Encoding Initiative. Springer Science & Business Media, 2012.

Pierazzo, E. "Encoding and Documenting Ancient Texts: The TEI Approach"

Pierazzo, E. "Textual Scholarship and Text Encoding". In *A New Companion to Digital Humanities.* S. Schreibman, R. Siemens and J. Unsworth). <https://doi.org/10.1002/9781118680605.ch21. 2015.>

Pfannenschmidt, Sarah L., and Tanya E. Clement. “Evaluating Digital Scholarship: Suggestions and Strategies for the Text Encoding Initiative.” Journal of the Text Encoding Initiative, no. Issue 7, Nov. 2014, https://doi.org/10.4000/jtei.949. Accessed 20 July 2020.

Susan Schreibman’s "Text Encoding in the Digital Humanities" In *A Companion to Digital Humanities, ed. Susan Schreibman*, Ray Siemens, John Unsworth. Oxford: Blackwell, 2004. https://companions.digitalhumanities.org/DH/

CHAPTER TWELVE

Teaching Interface As Cross-Cultural Metaphor

This chapter aims to teach students the importance of understanding metaphors in interface design and their cultural differences. Key learning outcomes include understanding metaphors, recognizing cultural differences, evaluating cross-cultural interface design, designing for diverse audiences, developing a critical perspective on design practices, implementing inclusive design principles, and understanding the impact of technology on culture. Activities include lectures, case studies, discussions, and research projects. The subject emphasizes the need for culturally aware design practices to create effective and inclusive user experiences. For a theoretical understanding of interface as a cultural construct, I prescribe Drucker's "Reading Interface," Kirschenbaum's "So the Colors Cover the Wires" Shneiderman's "The Eight Golden Rules of Interface Design," and Boor's "How Fluent is Your Interface?" for addressing the issues related to the importance of interface design as a culture and how software platforms are designed for the interface.

Teachers must enhance cross-cultural awareness and adapt traditional software development processes to create fluent interfaces for international markets, beyond just text and date/time formats. Internationalization and localization of a product require careful consideration of text, numbers, date, time, images, symbols, colours, flow, and functionality. During internationalization and localization, designers must consider various cross-cultural elements such as text, number, date, time formats, images, symbols, colours, flow, and functionality. The first two items are commonly considered, but the remaining items are often overlooked. Translating text into the local language is the first step, but it is more complicated than in a book. Translators must be familiar with the application domain and general human factors principles, such as screen layout and interactive behaviour design. Jargon should be eliminated during the internationalization step, as it is universally confusing and should be eliminated. Some computer-related terms do not exist in other languages, and translators should consider keeping the original terms for words that do not translate during localization. Character sets also need to be considered when designing applications. Many European languages contain a variety of characters with diacritical, such as *t+, & X*.

What is Interface?

An interface is a point of interaction or connection between different systems, components, or entities. It can have various meanings depending on the context, such as User Interface (UI), Application Programming Interface (API), Hardware Interface, Science and Engineering, General Use, Communication Interface, Client-Server Interface, and Interdisciplinary Interface. "Interfaces serve various purposes beyond these, such as entertaining, viewing, drawing, designing, playing games, exploring virtual worlds, and editing film and music. The establishment of 'interface conventions' has rapidly consolidated, but these conventions conceal underlying assumptions within their format and structure." (Kirschenbaum)

In technology and computing, an interface refers to how a user interacts with a computer or software application, such as screens, buttons, icons, and menus. In science and engineering, an interface is the boundary or surface where two different materials or phases meet and interact. In general use, an interface can refer to any point of interaction between different entities, such as people, organizations, or processes.

Communication interfaces describe methods or channels used for communication between individuals or groups, such as meetings, reports, or collaborative platforms. In business and social contexts, an interface might refer to the interaction between a client and a service provider, such as customer service platforms or support systems. In academia or research, an interface could describe the connection between different fields of study, such as data analysis with gender studies and law. Kirschenbaum's essay "So the Colors Cover the Wires" emphasizes the importance of understanding digital media by appreciating the physical hardware that supports and shapes digital experiences, challenging the notion that digital media is purely virtual.

Matthew Kirschenbaum's essay explores the complex relationship between physical and digital aspects of technology. He argues that digital media, often seen as intangible, is deeply connected to physical hardware, such as wires, circuits, and machinery. Kirschenbaum also discusses how digital experiences are mediated by physical technology, highlighting how the physical infrastructure of computers and devices shapes our interaction with digital content. He also examines the evolution of digital technology, highlighting how material conditions have changed over time and how these changes impact our interaction with digital media. The essay bridges theoretical discussions about digital media with practical considerations of hardware and software, demonstrating how theoretical concepts of media and technology are grounded in tangible realities. Teaching Ben Shneiderman's "Eight Golden Rules of Interface Design" involves engaging students with practical examples, interactive activities, and critical discussions. The structured approach includes an introduction to the principles, detailed explanations of each rule, and practical examples. Examples include consistency, shortcuts, informative feedback, dialogue design, error prevention, undo functionality, user control, and reducing short-term memory load. The goal is to improve usability and user experience in UI design.

Ben's Eight Golden Rules

Ben Shneiderman's "The Eight Golden Rules of Interface Design" are fundamental principles in user interface design, emphasizing the creation of user-friendly, intuitive, and effective interfaces. However, these rules have faced criticism for their generality, assuming a homogeneous user and cultural bias. The rules may not fully address the nuances of emerging technologies like touch interfaces and virtual reality.

User diversity is another concern, as the rules assume uniformity in user experience and cognitive abilities, overlooking the diverse needs and preferences of different users. Cultural bias can also lead to less effective or problematic interfaces in different cultural contexts. Balancing usability and aesthetics is another challenge, with some critics arguing that the focus on usability might overshadow the importance of aesthetic design.

Design constraints may limit creative or innovative design approaches, leading to interfaces lacking uniqueness or visual appeal. In dynamic and complex systems, strict following the rules may not always lead to the best design, necessitating more flexible and adaptive design approaches. Scalability issues may diminish the applicability of the rules, making additional principles and guidelines necessary for large-scale applications.

Modern UX design has expanded beyond Shneiderman's rules, incorporating considerations like emotional design, user journey mapping, and context-aware interactions. Critics argue that relying solely on the Eight Golden Rules might be insufficient for addressing broader aspects of modern UX design. Empirical evidence suggests that while the Eight Golden Rules are based on Shneiderman's research and experience, there may be a need for continuous validation and refinement based on current user research and usability testing.

William Boor's Theory of Fluency

William Boor's article "How Fluent is Your Interface?" discusses the concept of fluency in user interface design, emphasizing its importance for a smooth and enjoyable user experience. It outlines criteria for fluency, including consistency, feedback, error handling, and learnability. Boor emphasizes user testing and metrics to evaluate fluency and suggests design guidelines and continuous improvement to ensure smooth, predictable interactions. His article emphasizes the need for continuous improvement and user feedback. Fluency in UI design refers to seamless, intuitive interactions that align with users' expectations. It's crucial for a natural and enjoyable user experience. Key criteria include consistency, clear feedback, error handling, and learnability. Evaluating fluency involves user testing, metrics, and continuous improvement. Design guidelines and best practices are essential for achieving fluency.

Johanna Drucker's "Reading Interface": A Metaphor

Reading is a metaphoric act. Interface is a text. It reflects meaning. It is a metaphor. Johanna Drucker's essay, "Reading Interface," examines the relationship between reading and digital interfaces. It highlights the role of interfaces in shaping our reading experiences and interpretation of digital texts. Drucker also discusses the historical evolution of digital reading practices and the theoretical perspectives on interface design. She critiques challenges like screen fatigue and distraction but also highlights opportunities for innovation. Drucker advocates for a design approach prioritizing user experience and accessibility and calls for further research to enhance the reading experience. Johanna Drucker's essay, "Reading Interface," delves into the relationship between reading and digital interfaces, exploring how the design and functionality of interfaces affect our reading experiences and interpretation of digital texts.

1. Interface as a Medium

Reading Experience Metaphor

V. Evers's essay "Cross-Cultural Understanding of Metaphors in Interface Design" highlights the role of metaphors in simplifying user interactions across different cultures. Metaphors help users understand and interact with digital systems by mapping familiar concepts to digital environments. However, they can be culturally rooted and may not be universally understood. To create effective interfaces, designers should consider cultural differences and adapt their metaphors accordingly. This approach can enhance usability and user experience, making digital systems more intuitive and user-friendly. Digital interfaces represent cultural values and practices, shaping user experiences and interactions. Designers can create inclusive, representative digital environments by considering cultural reflection and power dynamics. Drucker argues that the interface itself plays a crucial role in shaping how we read and interact with digital texts. The design choices, such as layout, typography, and navigation, influence how readers engage with content and how information is processed.

Materiality of Interface

She emphasizes that digital texts are not just abstract data but are materially influenced by the interface through which they are presented. The interface mediates our interaction with the text, affecting our perception and understanding.

2. Visual and Interactive Design

Visual Representation

The visual aspects of an interface, including font choices, color schemes, and spacing, impact readability and user experience. Drucker discusses how these elements contribute to or detract from the effectiveness of reading digital texts.

Interactivity

Digital interfaces often include interactive features, such as hyperlinks, multimedia elements, and adjustable settings. Drucker explores how these interactive aspects can enhance or disrupt the reading process, influencing engagement and comprehension.

3. Historical and Theoretical Context

Historical Evolution

Digital interfaces as a metaphor allude to cultural representation that focuses on how Digital interfaces reflect, shape, and influence cultural values, norms, and practices. This perspective highlights the intersection of technology, design, and culture, emphasizing how interfaces are not just functional tools but also carriers of cultural meaning. Cultural reflection includes design aesthetics, symbolism, language, and localization. Cultural influences on user experience, technology, and design trends also shape interfaces. Globalization and localization challenges arise, and cultural critique and power dynamics can be addressed through inclusive design practices and cultural sensitivity training. Drucker places contemporary digital reading practices within a historical context, comparing them to earlier forms of text presentation, such as printed books and manuscripts. She examines how technological advancements have shifted the way we read and interact with texts.

Interdisciplinary Approach

She draws on various theoretical frameworks to analyze the relationship between text and interface, including media theory, cognitive science, and aesthetics. This interdisciplinary approach helps in understanding the broader implications of interface design on reading practices.

4. Critical Examination of Digital Interface

Drucker critically examines the challenges and limitations of digital reading interfaces, such as issues with screen fatigue, distraction, and the potential loss of deep reading skills. She considers how these factors impact the quality of reading and comprehension. Despite the challenges, Drucker also highlights opportunities for innovation in digital reading interfaces. She discusses how thoughtful design can improve readability, enhance user engagement, and support various reading practices. She suggests ways to improve digital reading interfaces by focusing on user needs, the context of use, and the nature of the content. She advocates for a design approach that prioritizes user experience and accessibility. She calls for continued research into the effects of interface design on reading and comprehension. This includes exploring new technologies and design strategies to better support diverse reading practices and preferences. By examining the visual and interactive aspects of interfaces, historical context, and theoretical perspectives, Drucker provides a critical analysis of how digital texts are presented and engaged. She highlights both the challenges and opportunities in digital reading, advocating for thoughtful design improvements and further research to enhance the reading experience.

Project Based on Eight Rules of Ben Shneiderman

Ben Shneiderman provides eight rules for interface design and graphic presentation: Strive for consistency, Seek universal usability, Offer informative feedback, Design dialogues to yield closure, Prevent errors, Permit easy reversal of actions, and Keep users in control.

1. Use consistent sequences of actions in similar situations, identical terminology, and colour, layout, and fonts throughout. Exceptions should be comprehensible and limited in number.
2. Design for plasticity, facilitating the transformation of content for diverse users. Add features for novices and experts, such as explanations and shortcuts, to enrich the interface design and improve perceived quality.
3. Provide interface feedback for every user action, with modest responses for frequent and minor actions and more substantial responses for infrequent and major actions.
4. Group actions into groups with a beginning, middle, and end, providing informative feedback after a group of actions.
5. Design the interface so that users cannot make serious errors, offering simple, constructive, and specific instructions for recovery.
6. Allow users to undo errors and explore unfamiliar options.
7. Provide simplified data-entry procedures, comprehensible displays, and rapid informative feedback to increase feelings of competence, mastery, and control over the system.
8. Designers should reduce short-term memory load by avoiding interfaces that require users to remember information from one display and use it on another. This includes avoiding re-entry of phone numbers, keeping website locations visible, and compacting lengthy forms for a single display.

Work upon these principles aim to increase user productivity through simplified data-entry procedures and comprehensible displays.

Reconsider How?

Russo Boor's article describes a cross-cultural checklist for text, local formats, graphics, symbols, colours, flow, and product functionality. An effective worldwide product development cycle is suggested. The suggested development cycle includes international design feedback and usability testing before product release. User interface designers must understand cross-cultural variations and adapt the software development process to build bridges. Creating international market-friendly interfaces goes beyond translating text and dates, times, and numbers. Instruct to inspire students to develop arguments on how Kirschenbaum said, "I have used the word 'interface' many times for referring to its cognitive effect because an interface is a medium for communication and exchange between two distinct worlds, beings, or systems. Its functionality is based on metaphors, such as "windows" and "desktop," which provide transparency and a workplace that emulates the physical world."

Catastrophic and Appropriate Interface

Matthew G. Kirschenbaum writes that the concept of interface, along with its related notions such as design and usability, is one of the most contentious topics in modern computing. Interface is commonly defined as the point of contact or interaction between two or more systems, equipment, or entities, often referred to as a surface or border. While these concepts promote the understanding of space, it is important to note that most interfaces also incorporate components related to time, touch, and cognition. "The steering wheel of a car, the control panel of a VCR, and the handle of a door are all instances of commonplace interfaces that demonstrate these characteristics." (Kirschenbaum) Within the realm of computers and computing, the term "interface" is commonly employed as a synonym for "graphical user interface" (GUI), which is predominantly encountered as a desktop Windows environment. It's wrong or poor implementation causes death too. He writes: "Interfaces are mostly discussed in mundane and utilitarian terms, but computing lore contains its share of instances where poor interface design has had lethal and catastrophic results. One notorious episode involved the Therac-25, a machine employed for cancer radiation therapy in the mid-1980s, whose cumbersome software interface contributed to several patient deaths from overexposure." (Kirschenbaum)

Doug Engelbart was a pioneering computer engineer and inventor who significantly influenced the development of interactive computing. His vision was to enhance human capabilities and problem-solving skills through technology. Engelbart's groundbreaking demonstration at the Fall Joint Computer Conference in 1968 showcased revolutionary concepts like the computer mouse, graphical user interface, hypertext, and collaborative tools. His work also led to the development of hypertext, which allowed users to link and navigate between information, and the NLS (oN-Line System), which demonstrated the potential of interactive computing. Doug Engelbart initially explored the use of physical components in the design of the mouse interface. Google Glass and augmented reality applications for portable devices are new advancements in user interface. The interface transitions beyond the screen and assumes a stratum of seen reality, and there are differences between digital and analogue interfaces. Question your students: How both the designs are examples of cultural construct? How does Doug Engelbart think of physical components of technology as a medium of interaction? And, assign some exercises:

Exercise 1 (In group)

Comment on the major phases in the development of interface design. And, analyse the following from cultural viewpoints:

- <http://en.wikipedia.org/wiki/History_of_the_graphical_user_interface>
- <http://www.catb.org/esr/writings/taouu/html/ch02.html>

Exercise 2 (Individual)

1. What are the required browser UI features? How do they compare to desktops? Links and continuities between these spaces?
2. Interfaces do not reveal what is "inside" the machine. Nor does it show how the computer works or processes data. Such processing is typically hidden by screens and surfaces. The environment is both hindering and beneficial. Examples to back this up? The issue of designing symbols that convey cognitive signals for actions that generate information architecture responses became apparent as the GUI progressed. What would your specialised software project icons represent? It takes engineering and creativity to imagine that digital items can mimic analogue operations. We "empty" a trashcan by clicking on it onscreen, which has little effect in real life, but we simply apply what we've learned on the computer. Standard interface dragging and dropping are not analogue. This leads us to conclude that the interface and physical world

are not aligned, but that altered expectations require cognitively and computationally efficient methods.

3. According to Matthew Kirschenbaum, the interface is a representation space, not a computer engine. Justify.
4. "By "information space," Johnson refers to the screen's transformation from a simple output device to a legitimate representational system, relying on visual acuity, interactivity, and direct manipulation.
5. One challenge in digital humanities endeavours is summarised in Jesse James Garrett's graphic, “Elements of the User Experience” Garrett claims that an interface can represent the design of knowledge/ information in a project or site or structure the user experience around site actions, but not both. Thus, when modelling intellectual content, you want to reflect the investment you made in your projects' elaborate structure and design in the interface. Your users‘ access to resources depends on whether you give them a list and index or a way to search, browse, view, read, listen, etc. Method 1 shows the knowledge model. Model user experience second.
6. Compare Garrett's diagram to other digital humanities projects mentioned in the previous chapters.
7. Apply Ben Shneiderman's eight interface design golden rules.

Attainments of Learning Outcomes

An interface is a model of intellectual content or instructions, combining presentation, representation, navigation, orientation, and network connections. It reflects user assumptions and models the difference between a consumer and a participant. Students learnt to create effective, inclusive, and culturally sensitive interfaces through comparative analysis, design workshops, user testing, and critical essays, preparing them for diverse global audiences.

If an intensive teacher training/FDP on TEI/ARBORTEXT/Students' placement training/expert lecture is required, contact the author at <valiur.bsb@gmail.com>.

Works Cited and Recommended Readings

Cooper, A. *About Face: The Essentials of User Interface Design.* Hoboken, NJ: John Wiley. 1995.

Drucker, Johanna. "Reading Interface" In *Visualization and Interpretation: Humanistic Approaches to Display.* The MIT Press, 2020.

Emerson, Lori. *Reading Writing Interfaces.* U of Minnesota Press, 2014.

Engberg, Maria, et al. *The Digital Reading Condition.* Taylor & Francis, 2022.

Kirschenbaum, M. G. "So the Colors Cover the Wires": Interface, Aesthetics, and Usability. 523-542. 2004. https://doi.org/10.1002/9780470999875.ch34

Shneiderman, B., Plaisant, C., Cohen, M., Jacobs, S., and Elmqvist, N., *Designing the User Interface: Strategies for Effective Human-Computer Interaction*: Sixth Edition, Pearson (May 2016) http://www.cs.umd.edu/hcil/DTUI6

Wong, Euphemia. "Shneiderman's Eight Golden Rules Will Help You Design Better Interfaces" Interaction Design Foundation - IxDF. 9 Sep. 2024 https://www.interaction-design.org/literature/article/shneiderman-s-eight-golden-rules-will-help-you-design-better-interfaces

Epilogue

This book opens hypothetical issues, and outsets the rejections. No issues, I aim to de-sediment the sand in water. Coming outside the comfort zone is not an easy task. It requires a challenge to the self first. *Teaching Students to Become Humanities Scientists: Breaking Tradition of Learning Divides through Digital Humanities* has navigated the complex and evolving landscape of integrating scientific approaches into the humanities. Throughout this book, we have explored how traditional disciplines within the humanities—such as literature, history, philosophy, and the arts—can benefit from and contribute to scientific methods and technological advancements. Our journey has underscored the potential for a transformative shift in how we teach, learn, and conduct research in the humanities.

The Evolving Role of Humanities Scientists

The concept of the "humanities scientist" represents a new paradigm where scholars and students alike blend rigorous scientific inquiry with deep humanistic analysis. This role involves not only employing quantitative methods, digital tools, and data analysis but also embracing the interpretative and critical approaches traditionally associated with the humanities. By integrating these methodologies, humanities scientists are uniquely positioned to address complex questions about human experience, culture, and history from multifaceted perspectives.

The Future of Humanities Science

Looking ahead, the field of humanities science will continue to evolve as new technologies and methodologies emerge. The role of the humanities scientist will become increasingly central in addressing contemporary challenges and fostering a deeper understanding of human culture and experience. As educators and researchers, it is our responsibility to adapt to these changes and to continually seek ways to enhance our teaching and research practices. The future of the humanities lies in our ability to remain dynamic and responsive to the shifting landscape of knowledge. By embracing an interdisciplinary approach, leveraging technological advancements, and upholding the core values of critical inquiry, we can contribute to a more nuanced and comprehensive understanding of the human condition.

Final Reflections

As *Teaching Students to Become Humanities Scientists: Breaking Tradition of Learning Divides through Digital Humanities* has aimed to provide a roadmap for integrating scientific and technological approaches into the study of the humanities, so it is serving. Feedback or reviews or critical responses to this book are welcomed at valiur.bsb@gmail.com. This integration not only enriches our research and teaching but also ensures that the humanities remain relevant and impactful in the modern world. As we move forward, let us embrace the challenges and opportunities that lie ahead, continuously seeking innovative ways to explore and understand the complexities of human experience. The journey of becoming a humanities scientist is one of curiosity, creativity, and dedication, and it is through this journey that we can hope to make meaningful contributions to both academic scholarship and societal understanding.

Thank you for engaging with this exploration of humanities science. May it inspire new ideas, foster collaboration, and contribute to the ongoing evolution of the field.

About The Author

Valiur Rahaman is an Associate Professor at Lovely Professional University, Punjab specializing in English Literature (Critical Theory-Deconstruction). With a background in Literature and Language, he has dedicated his career to advancing the integration of technology and critical thinking within the humanities. He has published extensively on topics related to digital humanities, pedagogy, and interdisciplinary research. He is committed to fostering innovative approaches to teaching and learning in the humanities and is actively involved in ADHO and ACH (USA) annual activities.

He is author of *Big Data Analytics in Cognitive Social Media and Literary Texts* (2021), *A Textbook on Databases in Digital Humanities* (2024), *Astitvarasa: An Aesthetics of Interrogation* (2017),*Acts of Literary Theory* (2016), and *Interpretations: Essays in Literary Theory* (2010). Readings are available at Amazon, Flipkart and Publishers' Websites. He has delivered expert lectures at many institutes of recognition in India and abroad. He teaches Literary Theory and Digital Humanities.

www.ingramcontent.com/pod-product-compliance
Ingram Content Group UK Ltd.
Pitfield, Milton Keynes, MK11 3LW, UK
UKHW041829200726
13854UKWH00002BA/902

9 798895 567890